ARCHITECTURE IN VIENNA
1850 TO 1930

HISTORICISM - JUGENDSTIL - NEW REALISM

BERTHA BLASCHKE & LUISE LIPSCHITZ

SpringerWienNewYork

Printed with support of MA 7,
Wissenschafts- und Forschungsförderung, City of Vienna

© 2003 Springer-Verlag/Wien
© of Figures: Springer-Verlag/Wien
Printed in Austria

Translation from German: Pedro M. Lopez
Layout: Loys Egg
Fotos by: Michael Zappe
Printing: A. Holzhausens Nfg., A-1140 Wien

Printed on acid-free and chlorine-free bleached paper
SPIN: 11504535

With numerous coloured Figures

ISBN 3-211-83735-3 Springer-Verlag Wien New York

Contents

The following is said to be true of historical rese-
arch: *"Generations define history − history defines
generations."* If applied to the history of architectural
style, the saying should read: *"Generations define
styles − styles define generations."*

By rule, there is a direct connection between historical occurrences and stylistic change. The two
major events that delineated the three architectural
styles discussed here (Historicism, Jugendstil, New
Realism), which also had a lasting influence on
Austria's history, both ran their course in March.
These were: the revolution of 1848 and the annexation of Austria by Germany in 1938. The situation
was somewhat different at the beginning of the
Secessionist movement, the Austrian variation of
Jugendstil. In this case, it was the waning artistic
vigor of the time that led to the rebirth of this
style. Its final end was again marked by a historical
event, World War I, between 1914 and 1918.

The revolution of March 1848 marked the beginning of the long-term demise of absolutism, which
was forced to make way for liberalism and therefore
for a gradual democratization − also in architectural matters. From an Austrian point of view, 1848
meant the end of the Hofbauamt's (Imperial Construction Authority's) omnipotence in all public
building matters and the beginning of competition.
Until then, architectural development had been
dictated from the top down, now democratization
began to set in. This made it possible for architecture to veer away from Biedermeier and Classicism
and to focus on Historicism, which was based on a
number of older styles that were molded into an
entirely new, unmistakable whole. The first building
discussed here, the Votivkirche, which takes its stylistic cues from Gothic architecture and from the

insights of the Renaissance, was the result of an architecture competition.

The annexation of Austria by Germany in March 1938 led to the end of any noteworthy construction in Austria. In Austria, the three most important styles in the period between the two World Wars – Expressionism, New Realism, International Style – are best described with the broader term of "Realism" here, since the Austrian versions are slightly distorted, diluted and stylistically impure. This development only continued after World War II, during the reconstruction period. The last building described here, the Arbeitsamt (Employment Office) Liesing, is the Austrian building of this period which formally comes closest to matching the international style of the time, although its light coloring represents a deviation from comparable buildings abroad.

The 100 buildings discussed here were constructed over a period of close to 80 years, between 1856 and 1932. Three generations of architects, which were mostly linked to one another through pupil-master relationships, created them. Otto Wagner (1841–1918), who developed into one of the Secession's leading architects after an early period defined by historicism, towered above the rest of this group. Wagner moved on to rationalism in his later work and thus paved the way for the emergence of Realism and maybe even for the "International Style".

The direct comparison between the first and the last buildings studied in this book, the Votivkirche and the Arbeitsamt Liesing, which are only separated by the relatively short period of one lifetime, emphasizes the enormous development within this era. A side-by-side matching of the Neo-Gothic religious building with the sober, purpose-built employment office, whose primary objectives are fulfilled via a purity of form combined with proportions that are carefully attuned to each other, provides enduring evidence of the revolution-like developments. Never before in the history of mankind did such radical change occur within the course of only a few years.

The development of Austrian architecture focuses on Vienna within the scope of time covered here. Within this context, Vienna was initially the imperial and royal capital and residence of a huge, variegated empire. After the collapse of the multicultural monarchy, Vienna became the federal capital of one of Europe's smallest countries. With few exceptions, both periods saw the construction of Austria's greatest architectural achievements. No other city allows for the tracing of developments and stylistic changes more clearly than Vienna. The larger part of the internationally recognized buildings in Austria, which had a Europe-wide influence in the history of architecture, were erected in Vienna.

They are all characterized concisely in this book and complemented with descriptions of perhaps lesser-known and less important buildings. This provides a broad spectrum, which also covers infrequently discussed buildings by architects such as Oskar Marmorek, Friedrich Ohmann, Josef Hackhofer and many others as well as the oft-cited projects by Hansen, Schmidt and Ferstel or Wagner, Hoffmann and Loos.

FIRST WALK - RINGSTRASSE

Districts I, II and IX

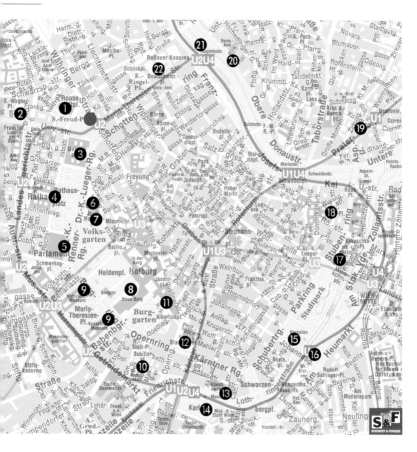

Districts I, II and IX

● **Point of departure:**
Schottenring at Jonasreindl Subway Station and Streetcar Stations

This walk takes you to the great monumental buildings lining the Ringstraße, on which construction commenced in 1857. These structures are followed by a number of buildings stemming from the post-historical period and the walk ends with Secession buildings. A very long walk awaits you, but you will have a story to be proud of when you return home and you will probably have achieved more than a number of Vienna's inhabitants.

It is best to begin the walk at the so-called Jonasreindl (Schottenring subway and streetcar station), which is named after Franz Jonas, a former mayor of Vienna. This important inner-city transportation hub at the Votivkirche was constructed during Jonas' time in office. A number of streetcar lines end here, busses and the U2 subway line all stop here as well. Since the walk literally takes you around the Ringstraße, you can also start your tour at any point on the route.

It is impossible to miss the imposing structure of the VOTIVKIRCHE (Page 32) as it emerges from behind the Sigmund Freud Park. The square was formerly named Maximilianplatz, after the protector of church construction, Archduke Ferdinand Maximilian (1832–1867), who took his place in history as the brother of Emperor Francis Joseph I and the unfortunate Emperor of Mexico, "Max of Mexico." The square bore the name Freiheitsplatz from 1920 until 1934, before becoming Dollfußplatz until 1938. It was designated Hermann-Göring-Platz from 1938 until 1945

❶
Votivkirche

I

before becoming Freiheitsplatz once again. It was then named after Franklin Delano Roosevelt (1882–1945), the president of the United States from 1933 until 1945.

Ferstelgasse, a street named after the architect of the Votivkirche, Heinrich von Ferstel skirts the back of the church and leads to Garnisongasse on the left, which you follow until you reach Universitätsstraße.

❷
Wohnhaus
Universitätsstraße

The WOHNHAUS UNIVERSITÄTSSTRASSE (Page 64) built by Otto Wagner is located on the corner of the street. After viewing the building, you can continue towards town again. This will take you directly to the UNIVERSITÄT (University) (Page 50) on Dr.-Karl-Lueger-Ring. Dr. Karl Lueger (1844–1910), was a former mayor of Vienna. This segment of the Ringstraße was known as the Mölkerring until 1920, before being named Franzensring. It was then named the Ring des 12. November, commemorating the founding day of the first Austrian republic. The location was then called Dr.-Ignaz-Seipel-Ring, after a former chancellor of the first republic and was referred to as Joseph-Bürckel-Ring between 1940 and 1945, after the NS provincial governor.

❸
Universität

If you pass the university walking along the Ringstraße, you reach Rathausplatz. As the name indicates, this is the location of the RATHAUS (City Hall) (Page 48). Finally, the antique Greek outline of the PARLAMENT (Page 46) looms, counterbalancing the university. This part of the Ringstraße is named after Dr. Karl Renner (1870–1950), the first federal president of the second Austrian Republic. Across from the Rathaus, on the other side of the Ringstraße still within the Dr.-Karl-Lueger-Ring area, lies the

❹
Rathaus
❺
Parlament

I

sprawling BURGTHEATER (Imperial Theater) (Page 52). An entry to the right leads to the Volksgarten Park. Right before you reach the Theseus temple, take a left and you will see the K A I S E R I N - E L I S A B E T H - D E N K M A L (Empress Elisabeth Memorial) (Page 112) that lies parallel to Löwelstraße, located behind the park. When you leave the memorial behind and move forwards, past the Meierei, a small former dairy housing a bistro, you exit the park and arrive at Heldenplatz, the site of historic events with the two imposing mounted statues of Archduke Carl and Prince Eugene created by Anton Fernkorn. The mighty crescent of the NEUE HOFBURG (New Hofburg Palace) (Page 56) rises at the foot of the two horsemen. The castle gate to the right takes you past the memorial to the Unknown Soldier, across the Burgring to Maria-Theresien-Platz, which is flanked on both sides by the KUNST-UND NATURHISTORISCHEN MUSEUM (Art History and Natural History Museums) (Page 44). The center of the square is reserved for a monument to Empress Maria Theresia.

Cross Babenbergerstraße behind the Kunsthistorisches Museum and continue along Opernring until you reach Robert-Stolz-Platz, a small square dedicated to the operetta composer (1880–1975). Take a right here and head to Schillerplatz, which is easily recognizable due to the large Friedrich Schiller monument. The AKADEMIE DER BILDENDEN KÜNSTE (Academy of Fine Arts) (Page 42), where Theophil Hansen, Carl von Hasenauer, Friedrich Ohmann and Otto Wagner all taught. After visiting the academy, it is best to return to Babenbergerstraße and then cross the Opernring

Burgtheater

Kaiserin Elisabeth-Denkmal

Neue Hofburg

Kunst- und Naturhistorisches Museum

Akademie der bildenden Künste

I

Glashaus

Staatsoper

Musikvereins-
gebäude

Stadtbahnstations-
pavillons

Wienfluss-
verbauung

either via the zebra stripes or the underground walkway. You are entering Burggarten from behind the New Hofburg. Now pass the Mozart Memorial before reaching the GLASHAUS (Page 82), which is visible beyond the meandering paths.

From there, leave Burggarten on a diagonal path towards Ringstraße, pass the Goethe Monument and cross Operngasse via another underground walkway before reaching the STAATSOPER (Page 34). It is advisable to cross to the other side of the street to enjoy a better view of the first building to go up on the Ringstraße. Stay on this side of the street and use the next underground walkway to avoid the heavy traffic on Kärntner Straße. Continue as if leaving town and take the first possible turn left into Bösendorferstraße before reaching Karlsplatz. After passing Adolf Loos' residence at Number 3 and the Künstlerhaus, you will see the MUSIKVEREINSGEBÄUDE (Music Association Building) (Page 38) at Number 12. From here, you can take a glance at the STADTBAHNSTATIONS-PAVILLONS on Karlsplatz (Page 76). If you still have time to spare, you can reach them directly with the help of an underground walkway (one of the pavilions is used as a coffee house, the other is occasionally the site of small exhibitions held by the Museum of the City of Vienna.

Walk straight up to Kärntner Ring, past the Hotel Imperial and cross Schwarzenbergplatz, with its equestrian monument featuring Prince Schwarzenberg. Continue along Schubertring before reaching Johannesgasse, and then turn right at this junction and walk up until you see the Stadtpark entrance. When you enter the park, you will see the WIENFLUSSVERBAUUNG (Wien River con-

struction) (Page 106) built by Friedrich Ohmann.
To the right, right after the entrance, lies the
STADTPARK STADTBAHNSTATION (Page
75) by Otto Wagner.

Once you return to Ringstraße, you continue
along Stadtpark and pass the famous Johann Strauß
memorial. Then you cross Weißkirchnerstraße
before reaching the MUSEUM and the UNI-
VERSITÄT FÜR ANGEWANDTE KUNST
(Page 40) at Stubenring 5. The equestrian statue of
Field Marshal Radetzky faces the government building, the next large building on Stubenring. His
outstretched hand points in the direction of the
POSTSPARKASSE (Postal Savings Bank) (Page
110) on Georg-Coch-Platz. Dr. Theodor Georg
von Coch (1842–1890) was one of the founders
of the Postal Savings Bank Office.

The route past the Urania over the Danube Canal
to Praterstraße Number 25 leads you to the
FÜRSTENHOF (Prince's Court) (Page 172),
which you can't miss. Walk back, but stay on the
same side of the Danube Canal. The view of the
city across the water will soften the blow of having
to walk up the heavily frequented Obere Donaustraße. The SCHÜTZENHAUS (Page 124) built
by Otto Wagner is located at Number 26. Continue
up the way on Obere Donaustraße until you reach
Augartenstraße. You can cross the Danube Canal
again at the AUGARTENBRÜCKE (Page 222).
Don't forget to take a look at the ROSSAUER
KASERNE (Page 36), which you will pass closely
in a few moments. You can choose between three
streets, either Hörl-, Kolingasse and Maria-The-
resien-Straße to thread your way up and back to the
point of departure for our walk, the Votivkirche.

⑯ Stadtbahnstation "Stadtpark"

⑰ Museum und Universität für angewandte Kunst

⑱ Postsparkasse

⑲ "Fürstenhof"

⑳ Schützenhaus

㉑ Augartenbrücke

㉒ Rossauer Kaserne

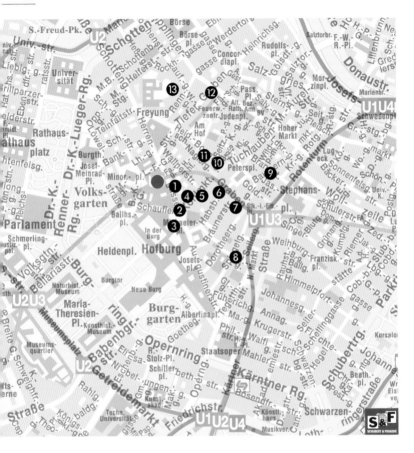

● **Point of Departure:**
Herrengasse U3 Subway Station

This walk will take you through Vienna's inner city. In the course of this excursion, you will see world-famous Secession period buildings and the city's first high-rise.

If you are staying outside the inner-city perimeter, it is best to take the U3 subway to Herrengasse Station. You can see the HOCHHAUS HERREN-GASSE (Page 232) as soon as you emerge from the station via the escalator (Herrengasse exit). Right next to it is the LOOSHAUS (Page 146), whose main façade faces Michaelerplatz and the generous semi-circle of the MICHAELERTRAKT HOF-BURG (Page 66). The history of this palace wing is very complex and its influence was of inestimable importance for the architecture of the Ringstraße. You will arrive at Kohlmarkt, the former coal market, after continuing right past the Looshaus. The street was certifiably referred to as "Am alten Cholmarkcht" (The Old Coal Market) as early as 1231. BUCHHANDLUNG MANZ (Page 162), which was designed by Adolf Loos, is located at Kohlmarkt No. 16. Diagonally across lies the ARTARIA-HAUS (Page 88), which is in a slightly recessed building on the sidewalk.

Walk down the Kohlmarkt and turn right onto the Graben. Although the Graben is a square today, it was actually a moat next to the city fortress wall between 1180 and 1190, before the city was expanded. The land was eventually filled and buildings were then constructed on the site. It served as a market square until 1753 and the first mention of the street name dates back to 1292.

Hochhaus
Herrengasse

Looshaus

Michaelertrakt,
of the Hofburg

Buchhandlung
Manz

Artaria-Haus

II

Schneidersalon
Kniže

Ankerhaus

Kärntner Bar

Zacherlhaus

"Zum Schwarzen
Kameel"

Engel-Apotheke

⑫
Hohe Brücke

The exclusive address at No 13 is fitting for SCHNEIDERSALON KNIŽE (Page 122). Otto Wagner's ANKERHAUS (Page 70), in which painter Friedensreich Hundertwasser kept a rooftop studio, is only a few steps away at No 10.

Keep walking and turn right into Seilergasse. You have to pay close attention now, since the next small alley is the Kärntner Durchgang, in which the KÄRNTNER BAR (Page 134) is located. Continue on towards Kärntner Straße and turn left once you're there. Keep walking until you pass Stephansdom and turn left into Brandstätte at the end of Stephansplatz. This part of the city was destroyed in 1276 after a great fire, which struck so much fear that the area remained undeveloped until 1560. The name "An der Prantstatt" ("At the site of the fire") was already in use in 1396. This historically significant street is the site of the ZACHERLHAUS (Page 108). Now you keep walking towards Tuchlauben, where you take a left and then continue until you turn right into Bognergasse. This was the seat of the Bogner family in earlier times, which is why the street was known as "Unter den bognern" as early as 1311. Stop at ZUM SCHWARZEN KAMEEL (The Black Camel) (Page 100) for a bite and enjoy the fin-de-siécle atmosphere. The richly colored mosaic portal of the ENGEL-APOTHEKE (Page 102) can be admired a few steps further up the street. Continue as if leaving town, pass Platz Am Hof and take a right downward to Tiefer Graben before reaching Freyung square. You can see the HOHE BRÜCKE (Page 104) in the distance as it arches over the narrow street below on Wipplingerstraße as you continue to walk out of town for another block. Take the next possible left at Renngasse, then the next right into Hohenstaufengasse. No 3 houses the distinguished historical LÄNDER-BANK (Page 60) façade designed by Otto Wagner. Only the interior of the building reveals its full splendor.

Länderbank

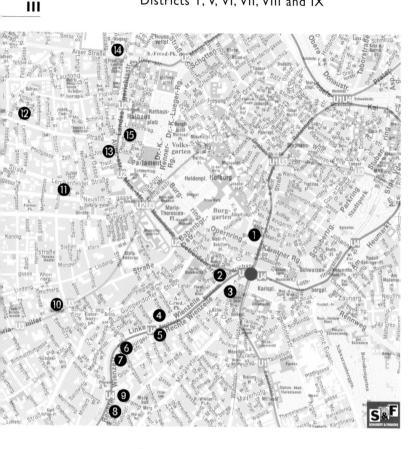

● **Point of Departure:**
Karlsplatz Subway Station

This walk will take you to Vienna's western districts. The first part of the route leads you past the buildings on the Wienzeile, which are grouped together closely, making it a comfortable walk. These are some of the earliest examples of Secessionist architecture in Vienna, but some of these buildings also break with those conventions, foreshadowing new stylistic developments. You can reach the SECESSION (Page 78) exhibition rooms on Friedrichstraße 12 best from either the STAATSOPER (Page 34) or the Karlsplatz subway station. After suffering major damage during the war and being reconstructed, the building was recently renovated and completely restored. The VERKEHRSBÜRO (Page 184), which was considered a retrograde structure by critics during its construction, is located directly across the street from the Secession. However, the building is of interest due to its technically sophisticated foundation over the Stadtbahn that arches over the Wien River. The route outwards on the busy Linke Wienzeile can be made more interesting if you walk through the rich variety of Naschmarkt stands, which are spread over the Wien River on a surface trussed with arched foundations. Urban planners originally conceived the Wienzeile as a splendid boulevard. Hence Otto Wagner reacted accordingly with his two WIENZEILEHÄUSER (Page 80) at No 38 and 40. Interestingly, he chose quarters for himself in a third, more modest building on Köstlergasse 3. Cross the Wienzeile at the end the Naschmarkt, in front of Otto Wagner's apartment houses and turn right immediately after the former KETTENBRÜCKEN-GASSE STADTBAHNSTATION (Page 74–77) (now a subway station) until you reach Steggasse and the twin residential block on STEGGASSE (Page 94) built by Josef Plečnik. The residential and commercial building "RÜDIGER-HOF" (Page 102) is another turret-like building located a few meters further away from town at Hamburgerstraße 20. The urban development situation

 Secession

 Staatsoper

 Verkehrsbüro

 Wienzeilehäuser

 Stadtbahn

 Steggasse

 "Rüdiger-Hof"

THIRD WALK

WIENTAL – NEUBAU – JOSEFSTADT

Districts I, V, VI, VII, VIII and IX

is particularly interesting here since the building is only a few steps away from both the Wien River and the large flow of incoming city traffic on Hamburgerstraße. The street name has nothing to do with the northern German city - Karl Hamburger (1848–1891) was a city councilor. Follow the curve of the river going further away from town until you reach Rechte Wienzeile 97, DRUCK- UND VERLAGSANSTALT "VOR-WÄRTS" (Page 144), printers and publishers. The site also served as the Austrian Social Democratic Party headquarters for decades and was a symbol thereof for many years.

❽
Druck- und
Verlagsanstalt
„Vorwärts"

Go back to Pilgrambrücke (named after Anton Pilgram, builder of the Stephansdom in the 16th century), cross it and continue past STADTBAHN-STATION PILGRAMGASSE (Page 75). Walk up Hofmühlgasse, which rises steeply and cross Gumpendorfer Straße before continuing upwards via Otto-Bauer-Gasse until you reach Mariahilfer Straße. Dr. Otto Bauer (1881–1938) was a leading Social Democratic politician during the period between the two World Wars. Turn right heading back into town until you see the high, black stone portal of the former ZENTRALSPARKASSE MARIAHILF-NEUBAU (Page 174) (today Bank Austria) designed by Adolf Loos. A longer, but more colorful way lined with many store windows takes you from Neubaugasse to Neustiftgasse. Take a right here as if heading into town and turn right again to reach the narrow alleyway of Döblergasse. Döblergasse got its name from the physicist Ludwig Döbler (1801–1846). The rational facades of the DÖBLERGASSE-NEUSTIFTGASSE apartement buildings (Page 142) are impressive samples of

❾
Stadtbahnstation
Pilgramgasse

❿
Zentralsparkasse
Mariahilf-Neubau

⓫
Miethäuser
Döblergasse-
Neustiftgasse

Otto Wagner's later work. Take the opportunity to visit the Academy of Fine Art's Otto-Wagner Archive, which is located in Otto Wagner's last apartment.

Head left as if leaving town on Lerchenfelder Straße, which intersects the other end of Döblergasse. Then turn right at Lerchengasse and head up to Josefstädter Straße. Or head down Kupkagasse from the other end and visit Hamerlingplatz and the NEUE WIENER HANDELAKADEMIE (Page 162) just a few steps away. Dr. Augustin Kupka (1844–1897) was a provincial councilor and Hamerlingplatz bears the name of writer Robert Hamerling (1830–1899).

⓬
Neue Wiener
Handelsakademie

Head back up to Josefstädter Straße and stroll down to Auerspergstraße. Turn right on Auerspergstraße until you reach No 9, the SANATORIUM LUITHLEN (Page 132). Turn around and look down Auerspergstraße and Landesgerichtsstraße, where you can see the gabled end of the WOHNHAUS UNIVERSITÄTSSTRASSE ("Hosenträgerhaus") (Page 64). Otto Wagner's MIETHÄUSER STADIONGASSE (Page 54) apartment buildings are visible on the other side of the large street crossing intersection (Josefstädter Straße, Auerspergstraße, Landesgerichtsstraße, Stadiongasse). Interestingly, the entrance to Stadiongasse 10 is actually at Rathausstraße 3.

⓭
Sanatorium
Luithlen

⓮
Wohnhaus
Universitätsstrasse

⓯
Miethäuser
Stadiongasse

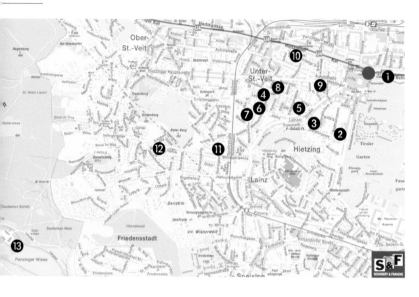

● Point of Departure:
Hietzing Subway Station, 60 Streetcar line,
Wenzgasse stop

Our fourth recommended walk takes you through
Hietzing, one of Vienna's most affluent districts.
You will cover large distances and you may even
have to take a bus to reach some of the buildings

in more remote locations, but the walks are brief and generally along streets with flanking gardens. Be willing to spend some time and make sure to take a snack or two with you since there are no stores or restaurants in some areas. Expect to spend a full day in the 13th if you include a visit to the Hermes-Villa in your walk.

The point of departure is Hietzing Subway Station, which no longer features the original Otto Wagner pavilion, removed in the sixties. However, the HOFPAVILLON DER STADTBAHN (Page 77) on Schönbrunner Schlossstraße is still intact and can be visited. Come back to the station after visiting it, turn left into Hietzinger Hauptstraße and pass Schlosshotel Schönbrunn. Then turn left into Maxingstraße after the church and the "Max of Mexico" memorial. Continue and take a right at Trauttmannsdorffgasse. The next left takes you to Wattmanngasse and WOHNHAUS WATTMANN-GASSE (Page 176), which is located at No 29. The building bears the nickname "chocolate house" due to its fetching brown majolica decor. The street bears the name of Prof. Josef Wattmann Freiherr von Maelcamp-Beaulieu (1789–1866), who was Kaiser Ferdinand I's personal physician. The narrow route of Tiroler Gasse intersects Wattmanngasse further up, continue and then take a right. Tirolergasse continues from here under the name of Gloriettegasse, in honor of the Gloriette building in nearby Schloss Schönbrunn Park that overlooks Vienna and was constructed between 1775 and 1780. Number 14–16 brings you to VILLA SKYWA-PRIMAVESI (Page 168) built by Josef Hoffmann. Continue along Gloriettegasse until you reach Lainzer Straße. The beginning of

Hofpavillon der Stadtbahn

Wohnhaus Wattmanngasse

Villa Skywa-Primavesi

IV

District XIII

❹
Haus Scheu

❺
Haus Beer

❻
Wohnhaus
Beckgasse

❼
Haus Steiner

❽
Haus Strasser

❾
Villa Wustl

Wenzgasse lies diagonally across Lainzer Straße. Walk into Wenzgasse a short way. HAUS SCHEU (Page 164) by Adolf Loos is located on the corner of Larochegasse. Karl Ritter von Laroche (1794–1884) was a court actor.

HAUS BEER (Page 224), built by Josef Frank, lies only a few steps away at Wenzgasse 12. If you are wondering who gave the street its name, it was Josef Wenz (1820–1892), civil engineer. Go back into Larochegasse, turn left at Elßlergasse and right again at the next street, Beckgasse. Max Wladimir Freiherr von Beck (1854–1943) was the Austrian Minister-President, during whose period of office universal suffrage was passed in Austria. Nummer 30 is the site of WOHNHAUS BECKGASSE (Page 86), which was built by Josef Plečnik. Follow Beckgasse until you reach the St. Veit-Gasse intersection. You will find HAUS STEINER (Page 150) built by Adolf Loos at No 10. Walk down St. Veit-Gasse towards the Wien River until you reach the Kupelwiesergasse intersection. Loos's HAUS STRASSER (Page 180) is located at number 28 on this street, which is named after the painter Leopold Kupelwieser (1796–1862). Continue downward via either Fichtnergasse or Stoessl-gasse until you reach Hietzinger Hauptstraße and then right and walk towards town again. You can see the garden side of VILLA WUSTL (Page 160) at No 40. You have to turn left at Braun-schweiggasse and take another left to Auhof-straße 13–15 in order to see the imposing dri-veway. Continue on Auhofstraße to Fleschgasse and turn right towards the Wien River before reaching Schließmanngasse at the next crossing. Number 11, with its inconspicuous façade is the site of HAUS RUFER (Page 188) built by Adolf Loos. Hans Schließmann (1852– 1920) was caricaturist and contemporary of Loos.

Haus Rufer

Now take the subway one station up from Unter St.-Veit to Ober-St.-Veit on the Hietzinger Kai. Take bus 54B to Tolstojgasse and then walk up to the Nothartgasse / Sauraugasse crossing. HAUS HORNER (Page 158), with its easily recognizable ceramic roof, is located at Nothartgasse No 7. Walk back to the bus station and take the 54B to Gobergasse / Jagdschloßgasse station. You are now standing in front of the WERKBUNDSIEDLUNG (Page 228) (Jagdschlossgasse 68−90 / Veitinger-gasse 71−117). Another ride on the 54B takes you to Ghelengasse, where you have to transfer to the 55B bus line. This will take you to the St. Veit gate of the Lainz Nature Park. Enter the park and walk through the well-kept grounds to the HERMES-VILLA (Page 58), where the Historical Museum of the City of Vienna hosts alternating exhibitions.

Haus Horner

Werkbund-siedlung

Hermes-Villa

FIFTH WALK

DÖBLING

District XIX

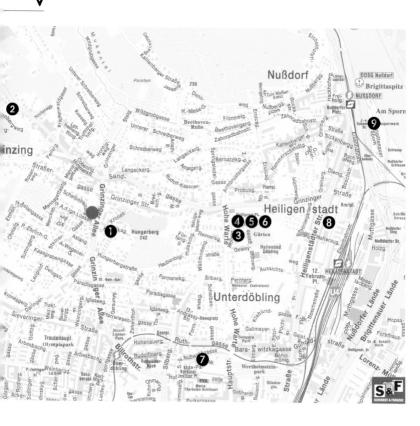

● **Point of Departure:**
Streetcar line 38 (An den langen Lüssen)

The fifth of our walks takes you to Döbling, Vienna's other affluent district on the northern edge of the city. As in Hietzing, villas are the main focus of this walk.

If you want to start from the center of town, it is

best to start from Schottenring, as was the case in our first walk. Get on streetcar 38 at the Jonasreindl and take it to one of the last stations, "An den langen Lüssen". The odd name comes from a deed for the plot dating back to 1315. A "Luß" was a plot of land won in a lottery. You are now on Grinzinger Allee. Number 50–52 is VILLA LEMBERGER (Page 170), the only building constructed by Jan Kotěra in Vienna. You can either take the streetcar one more stop or walk down to Grinzing. Get on the 38A bus, which also stops at the Grinzing streetcar station. Take the bus two stops to Cobenzl-gasse, which leads you to Schloss Cobenzl, built for Count Johann Graf von Cobenzl (1741–1815). Walk up a few more buildings until you reach HAUS HOCH (Page 154) at No 71. Built by Oskar Strnad and Oskar Wlach, it is one of the first buildings in Vienna to go beyond the Secessionist style of the day. Take the bus back down through Grinzing to Armbrustergasse / Hohe Warte station. Walk right and up to Hohe Warte until you reach Geweygasse. Follow the streetcar tracks of line 37 into Wollergasse, which was called Hohe Warte until 1894. A small dairy and coffee house were located here as of 1840, making the hilly area a popular stop for excursions. Franz Woller (1771–1839) was the owner of the Heiligenstadt baths. The "Villenkolonie Hohe Warte" is an ensemble of villas built by Josef Hoffman that spreads from Wollergasse to Steinfeldgasse around the right corner. HAUS MOLL II (Page 128) is at Woller-gassse 10. HAUS AST (Page 140) follows on the corner at No 12, with its other side facing Stein-feldgasse 2. HAUS SPITZER (Page 98) is next at Wollergassse 4. Two houses down, at No 6–8, lies

Villa Lemberger

Haus Hoch

Haus Moll II

Haus Ast

Haus Spitzer

27

FIFTH WALK

DÖBLING

District XIX

❻

Doppelwohnhaus
Moser-Moll I

❼

Haus Knips

❽

Karl-Marx-Hof

❾

Nußdorfer
Wehr- und
Schleusenanlage

the twin WOHNHAUS MOSER-MOLL I (Page
90). The street is named after the painter Franz
Steinfeld (1787–1862).

After visiting the "Villenkolonie Hohe Warte",
return to Hohe Warte and walk down (or take the
37 streetcar) until you reach the Ruthgasse / Barawitzkagasse intersection. Nußwaldgasse begins on
the right, immediately after Ruthgasse. Walk up this
street to HAUS KNIPS (Page 194) at No 22. The
street was given its name in 1824, since there used
to be many walnut trees in the area, although it was
also known as "Gemeindegasse" for many years.
Walk back to the Ruthgasse/Barawitzkagasse intersection and continue down Barawitzkagasse until
you reach Heiligenstädter Straße, or take bus 39A
one stop. Turn left on the wide Heiligenstädter
Straße and you will see the first block of the
KARL-MARX-HOF (Page 210) residential units,
which for tourism purposes is also known as the
more appealing "Kilometer of Art Deco". Take the
opportunity to walk through the huge courtyards
with their kindergartens and laundry rooms.
Absorb the atmosphere created by the imposing
1920's architecture and working class culture of
that period.

Grinzinger Straße begins at the end of the Karl-
Marx-Hof. Board the D streetcar and ride it for
one stop heading out of town. Get off at Sickenberggasse and walk right down this street towards
the Donaukanal. At Eisenbahnstraße, you will find
a walkway that takes you under the Franz-Josephs-
Bahn train tracks. From here you can see the
NUSSDORFER WEHR- UND SCHLEUSEN-
ANLAGE (Page 72), a weir and lock system that
is actually in Brigittenau, Vienna's 20th district

and not in Nußdorf. Otto Wagner's Josef-von-Schemmerl-Brücke bridge takes you over the Brigittenau spur. The appealing Biedermeier name of the bridge comes from Josef Schemmerl Ritter von Leytenbach (1752–1837), the engineer, bridge builder and proponent of the Wiener Neustadt canal.

ARCHITECTURE IN VIENNA

100 BUILDINGS

VOTIVKIRCHE
(PROBSTEIPFARRE ZUM GÖTTLICHEN HEILAND)

Heinrich von Ferstel

IX.
Rooseveltplatz

Sightseeing:
Open to the
public

Transportation:
Streetcar lines: 1, 2,
37, 38, 40, 41, 42,
43, 44, D,
Subway: U2
Bus: 1A
(Schottentor)

The Votivkirche was built in gratitude for the fai-
led attempt on Emperor Francis Joseph's life on
February 27, 1853. Archduke Ferdinand Max, the
emperor's brother (later Emperor Max of Mexico)
was named the church's protector.

An invitation to tender proposals for the building
was issued in 1854. The selection panel, which
included King Ludwig of Bavaria, selected the
design of 28 year-old Heinrich Ferstel from 75
projects. Ferstel's project included a four-pendant
dome calculated to achieve maximum effect at a
distance to suit the proposed site on a hill close to
the Belvedere. Ferstel later abandoned the idea of
using cupolas when the site in front of Schottentor

VOTIVKIRCHE
(PROBSTEIPFARRE ZUM GÖTTLICHEN HEILAND)

Heinrich von Ferstel

1856
1879

was finally chosen for the church. The cornerstone was laid on April 24, 1856 and marked the beginning of construction on the first example of strict historicism in Viennese religious architecture.

The building is surrounded by ample space on all sides and raised on a terrace. The impression of distance achieved is in accordance with its characteristics as a sacred building ("the church as an island") and memorial. The key guiding principle for the building's iconographic elements was its status as a memorial. Its significance was to be underlined by erecting memorials to many important men of the monarchy. This intention was actually only realized in the case of the mausoleum in honor of Count Niklas Salm, the defender of Vienna during the first Turkish siege of 1529.

Formally, the church was influenced by the ideal of the typical French two-tower cathedral with a choir aisle and orchestra pit. The building also has Baroque features, such as the fact that the exterior reflects the distribution of interior space.

STAATSOPER

Eduard van der Nüll
and August Siccard von Siccardsburg

I.
Opernring 2

Sightseeing:
Open
to the public

Transportation:
Streetcar lines:
1, 2, 62, 65, J, D,
Bus: 3A, 59A
(Oper)
Subways:
U1, U2, U4
(Karlsplatz)

The former imperial court opera was the first large-scale public building on the Ringstraße that was financed with funds from the city expansion fund. The design presented by Professors Eduard van der Nüll and August Siccard von Siccardsburg of the Imperial Academy of Fine Arts won the public competition held in 1860/61.

The structure is in the stylistic tradition of romantic historicism at its apogee and culminating moment. The two architects divided their work on the project, with one acting as the engineer and the other in charge of the design. Siccardsburg was responsible for the structural calculations of the building and van der Nüll took care of decorative matters.

The construction program required the administrative building and the theater structure to be one integral unit, which resulted in a drastic increase in the dimensions of the building. With its centrally located stage and audience space and the symmetrically organized stairwell blocks, foyers and administration wings, the opera shows a variety that calls to mind the complex ground plans of the late Classicist period. Terraced, intertwined front and side wings rise up to meet the flattened cupola of the building. A two-story balcony faces the Ringstraße. The ashlar stone wall structure evokes the classic forms of the Renaissance, i.e., references to 16th century Lombard, French and German architecture.

A period of strict historicism followed shortly after the building was completed. A humorous saying claiming the opera lacked style was coined during the time: *"Siccardsburg und van der Nüll – beide haben keinen Stil – Gotik oder Renaissance – ist den beiden alles ans."* (Siccardsburg and van der Nüll have no style, whether Gothic or Renaissance – it's all one and the same to them.)

ROSSAUERKASERNE

Colonel Karl Pilhal and Major Karl Markl

The leveling of all of the fortifications in the area that made construction possible was only approved in 1857, after the military authorities had finished their strategic planning for Vienna in reaction to the republican revolt of 1848. Two barracks, one new (formerly Kronprinz-Rudolph-Kaserne, now Rossauerkaserne) and the Franz-Joseph-Kaserne (built in 1854–57, torn down in 1902 and replaced in 1903 by Otto Wagner's Postsparkasse [Page 110]), were meant to create a triangle of fortresses to provide – it was said – protection *"for the highest members of the court against an uprising of the proletariat"*.

The location of the barracks north of the Augartenbrücke (Page 222) resulted from strategic and urban planning considerations. On one hand, the defensive barracks fortress was meant as the Kaiser-Franz-Josephs-Kaserne's counterpart, but the great amount of space required for military purposes (barracks and parade grounds) was at odds with the space available on the designated plot of land. Instead of entrusting architects with the construction of the giant complex, two officers were chosen

ROSSAUERKASERNE

Colonel Karl Pilhal and Major Karl Markl

1865
1870

for the job: Colonel Karl Pilhal and Major Karl Markl. Stylistically, the building was reminiscent of Italian castles, as were the Franz-Josephs-Kaserne and the Arsenal. Although the fortress was the last to be constructed, from 1865 to 1870, it was an exposed brick building like the other two complexes, and the most old-fashioned of the three with all of its structures grouped around its three courtyards. The complex's martial character is underlined by the ashlar stone at the corners and the windows, the sweeping lines and numerous turrets as well as by the richly decorated battlements.

MUSIKVEREINSGEBÄUDE

Theophil von Hansen

I.
Bösendorferstraße 12
Canovagasse 7
Karlsplatz 6
Dumbastraße

Sightseeing:
Scheduled events

Transportation:
Streetcar lines: J,
(Bösendorferstraße)
71, (Schwarzenberg-
platz)
Bus: 4A, Subway: U1,
U2, U4 (Karlsplatz)

The basilica-like building – a winning competition entry – was built on Karlsplatz between 1866 and 1869 in what was defined as "Greek Renaissance" style. Hence it represents a form of stylistic nexus in Hansen's work between the early Renaissance buildings (Palais Sina on Hoher Markt, Heinrichshof opposite the Opera and the Evangelical School on Karlsplatz) and the antique Greek Parliament (1871–1883) (Page 46). The Musikvereinsgebäude is part of a group of buildings that includes the Trade School and the Künstlerhaus. This unity is stressed by the alignment of the Künstlerhaus facing Karlsplatz from the middle with two other buildings facing it at right angles.

MUSIKVEREINSGEBÄUDE

Theophil von Hansen

The stringent organization of the ground plans and shear draft along with the elevation and frontispiece structure all achieve a dominance of the central building over the wing structures. The motif of the façade, with its central, three story gable-crowned pediment, the bottom two of which are outlined by rounded arches, is a reference to the façade of the Trade School across the way designed by Ferdinand Fellner the elder.

The large Musikverein hall, or "Golden Hall" is the central element of the entire building. The structure's pronounced nave is immediately apparent on the outside. The box seat caryatides that seem to support the balconies were set closer to the wall in 1911. As a result of the annual worldwide broadcast of the Vienna Philharmonic New Year's Concert, the "Golden Hall" is perhaps the world's most famous concert hall.

MUSEUM AND UNIVERSITÄT FÜR ANGEWANDTE KUNST

Heinrich von Ferstel, Ludwig Baumann, et al.

1867-1877

1907 1965

1989

I.
Stubenring 3–5
Weißkirchner-
straße 3
Oskar-Kokoschka-
Platz

Sightseeing:
Open
to the public

Transportation:
Streetcar lines: 1, 2,
Subway: U3,
Bus: 74A
(Stubentor)

In collaboration with the art historian Rudolf von Eitelberger Heinrich Ferstel built the Museum for Applied Arts (founded 1863) between 1868 to 1871 as the "k. k. Museum für Kunst und Industrie" (Imperial and Royal Museum of Art and Industry). It was the first museum built on the Ringstraße and became an example followed across Europe for other arts and crafts museums. The purpose of the structure was at the center of the museum's founding fathers' considerations from the very beginning. The object was to avoid merely exhibiting arts and crafts items by also creating a link to their manufacturing techniques. The three pillars of art, science and industry defined the Viennese arts and crafts museum. In accordance with the new artistic utilitarianism, Ferstel combined exposed brick Renaissance elements with a glass-steel construction method.

Rudolf von Eitelberger founded the University for Applied Arts in 1867 as the School of Arts and

MUSEUM AND UNIVERSITÄT FÜR ANGEWANDTE KUNST

Heinrich von Ferstel, Ludwig Baumann, et al.

1867-1877
1907 1965
1989

Crafts of the Austrian Museum for Art and Industry. Between 1875 and 1877 the building bordering the museum along the Stubenring was built according to plans by Heinrich Ferstel as well for the purpose of training specialists for both trade and the arts and crafts industry.

In 1907, the museum of arts and crafts was expanded (by Ludwig Baumann) on the Weißkirchnerstraße side in 1907 with a wing designed in the tradition of the Italian Renaissance. Much later, between 1960 and 1965 Karl Schwanzer and Eugen Wörle built an additional annex on Oskar-Kokoschka-Platz.

Specific structural changes took place at the museum complex as of 1989 (Peter Noever: MAK terrace level, Sepp Müller: connecting wing, Hermann Czech: café and restaurant, Walter Pichler: garden gate, Künstlergruppe Site: Ring Gate).

AKADEMIE DER BILDENDEN KÜNSTE

Theophil von Hansen

I.
Schillerplatz 3

Sightseeing:
Open
to the public

Transportation:
Streetcar lines:
1, 2, D, J,
(Burgring),
Subways: U1, U2,
U4
Bus: 57A
(Karlsplatz)

The Academy of Fine Arts is the oldest educational institution for artists in Austria. The building on Schillerplatz is the last public building constructed in Vienna while Theophil von Hansen was still teaching his special architecture class at the academy. Hansen had begun drawing up plans as early as 1869 at the request of the professorial college. The architect presented complete construction plans in March 1871, the reduced version of which was approved by the Kaiser on November 21st of the same year. Moving was completed by 1877, after the building's completion in 1876.

The building lies at the end of Schillerplatz in a lateral recess of the Ringstraße behind Schillerplatz. The structure's most striking feature is its clarity of disposition. Four wings surround a rectangular courtyard, divided in the middle by an open one-level aularian hall. The elevated, projecting pediment-like towers on balustrades constitute Hansen's variation of castle-type buildings. The long connec-

AKADEMIE DER BILDENDEN KÜNSTE

Theophil von Hansen

1871
1877

ting hallways face the courtyard, while the lecture halls, studios etc., face outwards.

The two lower levels were consolidated into one monumental block that is only interrupted by small round-arched windows and small rectangular mezzanine windows along the top level. The two identically designed upper levels feature round arches between relieved pilasters on the main facades (Schillerplatz, Getreidemarkt). Every second round arch is vitrified and the niches of the arches feature figure-shaped aedicules. The cube-like appearance of the building is given great surface plasticity by the layered wall structuring.

KUNSTHISTORISCHES AND NATURHISTORISCHES MUSEUM

Gottfried Semper, Carl von Hasenauer

I.

Burgring 5 und 7

Sightseeing:
See the respective
opening hours

Transportation:
Streetcar lines:
1, 2, D, J,
Bus: 2A, 57A,
(Burgring)
Subway: U2
(Museumsquartier)

In 1866, Heinrich Ferstel, Theophil Hansen, Carl Hasenauer and Moriz Löhr were invited to draft layouts for the planned imperial museums. The bid description included the purpose and location of both museums. None of the projects received a direct recommendation for completion when the jury handed in its decision in 1867. After intense public debate, Europe's most respected architect of the period, Gottfried Semper, was consulted in order to bring new inspiration to this central Ringstraße project. Semper presented complete plans that connected the Hofburg (Page 56) and the museums into one joint complex, the "Kaiserforum." He chose the still youthful Hasenauer as his associate for the project.

Both buildings were constructed in Neo-Renaissance style on rectangular ground plans with two large inside courtyards in each museum. In deference to the demands of historicism, the link between the past, present and future, the intention was to converge the exhibits and the museum space into

KUNSTHISTORISCHES
AND NATURHISTORISCHES MUSEUM

Gottfried Semper, Carl von Hasenauer

one unit. The Kunsthistorisches Museum also expressed this precept in its architecture by striking a religious note of order. The five cupolas covering the central structures (middle cupola with five satellites) are clear evidence of this direction. Semper was largely responsible for the exterior of the museums, while Hasenauer was in charge of the interiors, for which acclaimed Viennese painters such as Hans Makart and the young Gustav Klimt were commissioned.

Emperor Francis Joseph I opened the Naturhistorisches Museum in 1889, and likewise the Kunsthistorisches Museum in 1891.

PARLAMENT
Theophil von Hansen

Sightseeing:
Visiting available
on request

Transportation:
Streetcar lines: 1, 2,
D, J, (Stadiongasse)
Subways: U2
(Lerchenfelder-
straße)
U3 (Dr.-Karl-
Renner-Ring)

It is assumed that because Theophil Hansen lost the imperial museum competition the Kaiser entrusted the construction of the Parliament to him. There was no competition for the project and it seems to have been given to him as compensation. The site of the new building was to be the exercise and parade grounds of the Josefstadt Glacis. The new Rathaus (Page 48) would be built in the middle, flanked by the Parliament and the University (Page 50). The architects of these buildings, Schmidt, Hansen and Ferstel were required to coordinate and agree on the exact location of the three monumental buildings.

In 1869, the new political situation forced Hansen to re-design his for the upper house of the Parliament to include both the upper and lower house in a single building. With his sketch of the integrated upper and lower houses, Hansen submitted an explanation that stressed his effort to create the impression of one level and the importance of the central section and its portico.

For the entrance Hansen designed a monumental

PARLAMENT
Theophil von Hansen

fountain featuring a column. The tip was meant to bear an allegory for "Austria" with the main rivers of the monarchy at its feet. The fountain was ultimately built with a Pallas Athena statue in 1898. The selection of antique forms for the parliament building was a programmatic decision. It was meant as a link to the Greek democracies. However, it was also based on the broad classicist currents of that time.

Max Fellerer and Eugen Wörle restored the building in 1955/56 after it suffered damage during WWII.

RATHAUS
Friedrich von Schmidt

I.
Rathausplatz |
Felderstraße |
Friedrich Schmidt-
Platz |

Sightseeing:
Open
to the public

Transportation:
Streetcar lines: 1, 2,
D, Subway: U2
(Rathausplatz,
Friedrich Schmidt-
Platz)

In the mid-19th century, it was decided that the old Vienna City Hall on Wipplingerstraße would be vacated and space was sought to build a new one. The plot on the Stadtpark was only purchased in 1867 and the competition for the required construction plans was announced the following year. The invitation to enter a bid was issued to all *"domestic and foreign experts."* One of the 64 projects submitted was that of Friedrich Schmidt, a Swabian cathedral architect, which ultimately won the competition.

Schmidt designed a Gothic building, which even at a distance had to, as he said, *"correspond with the traditional building types of the epoch that saw the blossoming of German citizenry."* This was an allusion to the large number of late gothic city halls in Germany and Flanders that had been built by the burghers there as a visual reminder of the ever-increasing strength of their position with regards to their feudal masters. However, the ground plans and base course of the building are unthinkable without Renaissance and Baroque influences.

RATHAUS
Friedrich von Schmidt

Viennese mayor Kajetan Felder finally succeeded in securing the
Kaiser's blessing for the removal of the exercise and parade grounds on the Josefstädter Glacis, which provided him with the desired site. Together with the Burgtheater (Page 52), Parliament (Page 46) and the University (Page 50), the City Hall creates one of the most beautiful ensembles of urban buildings on the Ringstraße.

On September 12th, 1883, Emperor Francis Joseph I personally set the last stone, marking the end of construction. The raising of the 3.4-meter high "Rathausmann" a copper standard bearer weighing 1.8 tons to its lofty perch at the tip of the tower was the culminating event of the ceremony.

UNIVERSITÄT
Heinrich von Ferstel

I.
Dr.-Karl-Lueger-
Ring I

Sightseeing:
Open
to the public

Transportation:
Streetcar lines: I, 2,
37, 38, 40, 41, 42,
43, 44, D,
Subway: U2
Bus: I A
(Schottentor)

In 1854, Emperor Francis Joseph commissioned Eduard van der Nüll and August Siccard von Siccardsburg, the architects of the Imperial Opera (Page 34) to design a cité universitaire project on the square behind Votivkirche. A construction committee advised by Heinrich Ferstel as the technical consultant then elaborated the definitive program, in which the desire for separate institute buildings was taken into consideration. Only the chemistry laboratories (IX. Währinger Straße 10), the anatomical physiological and the embryology institute at the Währinger-Schwarzspanierstraße (IX., Währinger Straße 11–13) corner were actually completed according to the original plan.

Heinrich Ferstel was commissioned for the hitherto unheard of Herculean task of building an entire university complex for four faculties including a library, offices, lecture halls, ceremonial halls and residential units. His first proposal already included comprehensive ground plan solutions. The second

UNIVERSITÄT
Heinrich von Ferstel

project also featured corner pavilions in order to achieve a more forceful, massive appearance. Ground plans were very important to Ferstel. The system of courtyards around which the different room types are grouped and the communication system formed what Ferstel called the *"skeleton"* of the complex. On the outside, this was stressed with the nuanced stories. Ferstel's use of recessed and projecting surfaces along the long fronts gives the structure impressive silhouettes. He was alluding to Renaissance and Baroque forms in a conscious allusion to the period that had seen the high point of the humanities. The architect's design of the arcades is based on the Palazzo Farnese in Rome. It was meant as a memorial park in honor of famous university professors and as a recreational space for students.

BURGTHEATER
Gottfried Semper, Carl von Hasenauer

I.
Dr.-Karl-Lueger-
Ring 2

Sightseeing:
Open
to the public

Transportation:
Streetcar lines:
1, 2, D
(Burgtheater)

By the mid 19th century, the old Hofburgtheater on Michaelerplatz was proving increasingly inadequate to meet the rising demand for entertainment. At this time, the cathedral architect Leopold Ernst painted a watercolor of a new theater on Ballhausplatz. However, the first plan for the new Burgtheater only came from Gottfried Semper in June 1869 as part of the Kaiserforum project. The basic exterior form was decided on by April 1870. The square opposite the Rathaus (Page 48) was chosen for the new building.

Semper followed his design for the Dresden Opera House in planning the Burgtheater. The convex central pediment structure with the triaxial central loggia Hasenauer had insisted on against Semper's will, includes the audience space and the respective stairways. The stage wing can be distinguished from the audience space by its roof shape. The two imposing lateral staircases were added to counterbalance the broad façade of the Rathaus (Page 48). Semper cited the forms of the Italian High Renaissance in his exterior design.

The structure's outer walls feature hundreds of

BURGTHEATER

Gottfried Semper, Carl von Hasenauer

1874
1888

plastics, which depict the world's famous dramatic writers and figures of the theater.

The theater's interiors bore Hasenauer's signature, he designing them with sumptuous Neo-baroque furnishings. The roof paintings of both ceremonial staircases were painted by a "company of artists" including the brothers Gustav and Ernst Klimt and Franz Matsch.

The lyre-shaped audience pit was rebuilt in a horseshoe form in 1897 to improve the theater's acoustics.

MIETHÄUSER STADIONGASSE
Otto Wagner

1880
1883

I.
Stadiongasse 6–8,
Rathausstraße 3,
Stadiongasse 10

Sightseeing:
None

Transportation:
Streetcar lines: J,
Subway: U2
(Rathaus)

Otto Wagner acted as his own contractor for these two buildings, as was the case with most of his projects. This step gave him almost unrestricted control in realizing his vision of contemporary buildings. Ludwig Hevesi summed up the stylistic development of the apartment buildings Wagner built up until 1900 in a concise characterization: *"A number of apartment buildings were constructed then: Rathausstraße 3, Stadiongasse 6–8, Schottenring 23, the block of buildings at the beginning of Rennweg, the group of houses at the corner of Wienzeile and Köstlergasse etc. Initially, they were variations on later Renaissance themes, although they show greater freedom of spirit and a thorough sense of purpose. New ideas only broke with the old forms at the beginning of the nineties."*

In his notes on Stadiongasse 6–8, Wagner wrote: *"And so a simple and I think practical ground plan distribution was achieved, resulting in apartments that are suitable to this quarter and its tenants. Of course the interior furnishings and individual constructions are in keeping with the corresponding demands. Hence*

MIETHÄUSER STADIONGASSE
Otto Wagner

the vestibules are Untersberg marble monoliths, the steps are Karst marble and the very large hallway windows are made of iron with patterned window panes, brass was used for the wall lighting fixtures..."

Wagner furnished an apartment on the main floor of the building in 1886. The almost oppressively sumptuous décor makes it hard to believe that the architect would change his style drastically in a few years and become one of the fathers of modern architecture at an advanced age.

NEUE HOFBURG
Gottfried Semper, Carl von Hasenauer,
Emil Ritter von Förster, Friedrich Ohmann

I.
Heldenplatz

Sightseeing:
During opening
hours

Transportation:
Streetcar lines:
1, 2, D, J,
Bus: 57A
(Burgring)

Gottfried Semper was consulted in order to resolve
the problems surrounding the construction of the
two imperial museums. He re-directed planning
away from building on the suburban side of the
complex and emphasized planning an entire Hofburg museum complex, a "Kaiserforum." He was
entrusted with the general supervision of planning
by the Kaiser, bearing in mind that he was expec-
ted to use the projects that had been handed in
during the competition held earlier. Semper chose
Hasenauer's project and also became his associate.
Semper's main was concern was that, *"the imperial
Hofburg becomes the commanding central point of
the entire estate, in which everything else refers and
is subordinated to it."*
It was possible to begin to work on the execution
of Semper's plans for the new Hofburg in 1878.
Carl von Hasenauer oversaw construction from
1883 until 1893 and he saw the building outline rise
above street level by 1890. However, Hasenauer
passed away in 1894, before construction was complete.
After Hasenauer, Emil Ritter von Förster was given

overall supervision of the project and he introduced a number of changes to the layout during construction. It is obvious that the thought of abandoning plans to build a second palace wing and connecting structure and thus give up the "forum" concept was an issue by 1898. Finally, Friedrich Ohmann was called from Prague to master the problems on a construction site that faced more bureaucratic than artistic difficulties. He made the lateral wing from the central building to the Imperial garden wing over the two Fernkorn monuments the main axle of the project. Since Archduke Francis Ferdinand disagreed with this idea, Ludwig Bauman was appointed to succeed Ohmann.

HERMES-VILLA
Carl von Hasenauer

"How did it ever occur to you to name a house after the patron of travel, Sisi? It doesn't make any sense?", asked Kaiser Francis Joseph of his wife. She responded: *"That's exactly why, I want to remind myself that I never want to be bound to a place or forced to stay anywhere when I am within these walls."* (Empress Elisabeth in her diary, February 1887)

XIII.
Lainzer Tiergarten

Sightseeing:
During opening hours

Transportation:
Bus: 60B
(Lainzer Tor),
Bus: 55B
(St. Veiter-Tor)

The Hermes-Villa lies in the middle of the former imperial hunting grounds, now the "Lainzer Tiergarten." At the request of Kaiser Francis Joseph, they were laid out according to the Ringstraße architect Carl von Hasenauer's plans between 1882 and 1886. The Kaiser had the villa designed as a hunting lodge and gave it to his wife hoping she would find a lasting private sanctuary. He referred to it as, "our retreat for our later years."

The entire ensemble is set in the landscape convincingly. The playful distribution of the system of buildings, or asymmetry, became an example followed by later romantic villas. Stylistically, it was built as a mix of Renaissance and Baroque forms.

HERMES-VILLA

Carl von Hasenauer

Along with Carl von Hasenauer, the Kaiser also hired two other artists for whom he had great esteem: Viktor Tilgner as the sculptor and Hans Makart as the painter. Elisabeth's bedroom bears testament to the art of interior decoration in Makart's time with its "Midsummer Night's Dream" theme. Empress Elisabeth commissioned the young Gustav Klimt together with his brother Ernst as well as Franz Matsch for the ceiling painting in her salon.

LÄNDERBANK
(today: public administration)

Otto Wagner

Hohenstaufen-
gasse 3

Sightseeing:
none

Transportation:
Streetcar lines:
37, 38, 40, 41,
42, 43, 44
Subway: U2
(Schottentor)

The administration building of the private "k. k.
priv. österreichischen Länderbank" is an example
of Otto Wagner's early work that shows very clear
retrograde references to historical styles. He made
use of Renaissance styles and forms on the façade
and on the inside, which was the case with many
of his projects during this period of his work.

Aside from the Renaissance-style reception, Wagner
built the first modern office building in Vienna
whose layout, section and courtyard facade still
attract unreserved admiration today. Although the
street façade reveals little of the revolutionary building gem, the interiors, with the use of glass floors,
glass roofs and light office separation panels and
its brilliant layout compose a symphony of space.
With great skill, Wagner erected a building on the
uneven site with a circular vestibule that compen-

sates and simultaneously absorbs the fractious axial sequence of the rooms.

With baffling, simple means, Wagner created interiors with a religious effect; similar to those he designed for the Postsparkasse hall two decades later (Page 111). Otto Wagner wrote the following about the building: *"The exacting air and light requirements, connecting rooms making it easy to find them quickly and the fact that a bank's business can expand in one direction or the other made simple office redistribution possibilities desirable. The architect recognized this need and made use of a central distribution layout on all levels."*

VILLA WAGNER I
Otto Wagner

Sightseeing:
Prior booking
required

Transportation:
Streetcar line: 49
(Hütteldorf,
Bujattigasse),
Bus: Regional bus
148, 152

Otto Wagner built himself a generously sized suburban villa on the edge of the woods in Hütteldorf
as his own private residence. He constructed it
after his second marriage in 1881 and intended to
use it as a summer house. For Wagner, the building
was a symbol of his restored sense of family balan-
ce after the failure of his first marriage in 1880. In
contrast to the Hermes Villa (Page 58) Hasenauer
had built only a few years earlier, Wagner's villa is
dominated by a sense of symmetry. The only con-
cession to the new tendencies in architecture was
the use of iron banisters on the imposing Pre-
secessionist style staircase. The building lies on a
slope and consists of the square central structure
flanked by two pergolas. Hence the building opens
its breadth to nature. The central axle of the building reflects this with the integration of the loggia,
defined by four massive columns with its surroundings. Once again Wagner resorted to the "free
Renaissance style" he had used in building the
Länderbank. *"His early period under the influence*

VILLA WAGNER I
Otto Wagner

of styles nonetheless has its own personal coloring. He developed a free Renaissance and free Baroque style that prove he did not submit to the constrictions of one direction…" (Joseph August Lux)

Originally the greenhouse, the right pergola was fitted with glass and furnished as a large billiards room in 1895. The left pergola was re-fitted as a studio in 1899, including a painting on glass by Adolf Böhm, one of the founding members of the Secession (Page 78).

WOHNHAUS UNIVERSITÄTSSTRASSE
„HOSENTRÄGERHAUS"

Otto Wagner

IX.
Universitäts-
straße 12
Garnisongasse 1

Sightseeing:
None

Transportation:
Streetcar lines:
43, 44
(Universitätsstraße)

Otto Wagner acted as his own contractor once again on this building for affluent tenants, as had been the case with the projects on Stadiongasse (Page 54), on Rennweg (Page 68), on Wienzeile (Page 80) and on Döblergasse (Page 142). The three-front building is of great importance in terms of urban construction due to its exposed site on the gable end of Landesgerichtsstraße, which runs straight past the end wall of the building and the double corner on Garelligasse and Garnisongasse, where the entrance is located. This sight axis gave Wagner reason to use vase-shaped applications and a decorated roof crest, which gives the building an individual silhouette. The vertical, almost smooth Lisene edging its Neo-Baroque stucco decor en-

WOHNHAUS UNIVERSITÄTSSTRASSE

„HOSENTRÄGERHAUS"

Otto Wagner

couraged the Viennese to refer to it as the *"Haus mit den Hosenträgern"* (house with suspenders) at the time. Wagner's use of such smooth edging throughout the building signaled the first departure from the "palace scheme" (emphasis on the second floor) in Viennese apartment house building, by letting the building's construction elements become visible. At the same time, he also stressed the structure's vertical aspects with the small axis of the windows, making the building one of the first high-rises linked to the Chicago School of architecture. The apartment house does achieve a more slender appearance than the earlier buildings in Wagner's oeuvre. The basic sequential horizontal lines covering the entire house can also be recognized at the building's corners, compensating for the dominant vertical structuring.

The layout is the same as that of the building on Rathausstraße 3/Stadiongasse 10 (Page 54) with the windows of the semicircular staircase looking down on a courtyard. Two noteworthy features are the nearly square foyer and the wide, extremely shallow stairs. There are only two well-appointed 350 square-meter apartments on each floor.

MICHAELERTRAKT DER HOFBURG

Ferdinand Kirschner according to plans
by Joseph Emanuel Fischer von Erlach

I.
Michaelerplatz I

Sightseeing:
Open
to the public

Transportation:
Bus: 2A, 3A
(Michaelerplatz)
Subway: U3
(Herrengasse)

Hope that new, independent ideas could be introduced for the Michaelertrackt wing of the Hofburg
rose until the presentation of Semper's Kaiserforum
around 1869/70, when it became clear that the
same concept behind the Hofburg expansion "Ur-
projekt" (original project) begun under Karl VI
had to be followed. This meant adherence to the
tradition set down in the plans by the revered
Johann Bernhard Fischer von Erlach, mere frag-
ments of which were executed by his son Joseph
Emanuel. The wing's torso had dominated the
Michaelerplatz since 1737. Discussion began over
the distribution of the existing Baroque plans and
an engraving by Salomon Kleiner that shows a uto-
pian complete project. The fight concentrated on
whether a cupola had been planned or not and if
so, if only one was enough or were more needed?
Finally, Captain Ferdinand Kirschner proposed a
compromise that included a striking high central
cupola with a curved façade. This suggestion was
approved by most of the experts and the main
contractor, the Kaiser.
Excavation and foundation work for the building

MICHAELERTRAKT DER HOFBURG
Ferdinand Kirschner according to plans
by Joseph Emanuel Fischer von Erlach

began after the old Burgtheater (Page 52), which had projected from the Michaelerplatz's torso, was leveled in 1888. The two Michaelerkuppel cupola domes were built as light steel frames using the most modern construction technology available at the time.

The two mighty wall fountains on the flanks show "Austria's Maritime Sovereignty" (by Rudolf Weyr) and "Austria's Sovereignty on Land" (by Edmund Hellmer).

MIETHÄUSER RENNWEG
Otto Wagner

III.
Rennweg 1a, 3, 5
Auenbrugger-
gasse 2

Sightseeing:
None

Transportation:
Streetcar line: 71
(Unteres
Belvedere)

Otto Wagner acted as his own contractor again between 1889 and 1891, when he built three Rococo style buildings on a plot of land on Rennweg as, *"a charming Baroque composition"* (Joseph August Lux). Otto Wagner chose the middle building of this important example of urban architecture as his family's home and the site of his studio. This studio palace is framed by the apartment buildings on each side. Wagner's studio is on the ground floor. The first floor contained the representation area including the dining room, salon and a room intended for the head of the household. The second floor was reserved for the children's room and bedrooms. Otto Wagner kept his studio here until he was given a chair as professor of the Special School of Architecture at the Academy of Fine Arts in (Page 40) 1894. Wagner later sold the house to Countess Hoyos, the widow of the painter Friedrich Amerling. It is therefore still called "Palais Hoyos" today, although it now houses an embassy.

The corner apartment building at Rennweg 1a is completely disfigured on both the outside and inside. The rounded edge of the building facing

MIETHÄUSER RENNWEG

Otto Wagner

Schwarzenbergplatz shows Wagner's attempt to find an adequate urban construction solution.

Right after it was completed, the composer and opera director Gustav Mahler moved into an apartment in the corner building at Rennweg 5, whose entrance is located at Auenbruggergasse 2.
The design of both apartment buildings is far simpler than that of Wagner's house.

ANKERHAUS
Otto Wagner

I.
Graben 10
Spiegelgasse 2

Sightseeing:
None

Transportation:
Subways: U1, U3
(Stephansplatz)

"Der Anker" insurance company contracted Otto Wagner to plan an apartment and office building in 1894. One of the project's special features was the fact that it was free standing on the three sides facing Spiegelgasse, Graben and Dorotheergasse. This confronted Wagner with a similar architectural situation to that of the apartment building on Universitätsstraße (Page 64). Although a continuation of the Spiegelgasse building with a second apartment house, a "Wienerhaus" (Viennese building) had been planned, an enlarged variant of the "Der Anker" building was finally constructed.

The two-story business area and the glass roofing

ANKERHAUS

Otto Wagner

for a photo studio are remarkably early examples of a metropolitan architectural attitude.

"Der Architekt," an architectural digest of the time analyzed the building in 1896: *"The basic principle of building everything based on the respective requirements and completing it with aesthetic design as well as the use of the most modern construction materials and the exhibition thereof…is also expressed clearly here…*

Two identically large, elliptical staircases that lie at equal distances to the sole building entrance support communication within the building…

The business portal that spans both the ground floor and mezzanine was completed with an architecturally effective wrought iron balcony banister. The portal dissolves into columns that are grouped together to create the clear lines of the plaster façade.

The marked emphasis on all constructive elements, the visible traverse and the generous use of Mannstädt iron on the façade as well as the clear symbolism of the sculpted ornaments bear testament to the modern-realist tendencies of the architect."

NUSSDORFER WEHR- UND SCHLEUSENANLAGE

Otto Wagner

XX.
Am Brigittenauer
Sporn 7

Sightseeing:
Open
to the public

Transportation:
Streetcar line: D
(Sickenberggasse),
City Rail: S40
(Nussdorf)

The railway line and sewage pipes along the Danube Canal made a dam necessary at the beginning of the canal. The enormous effort Wagner put into the facility by drawing 1500 layouts up until 1898 shows how important the dam was to him. This example of his work shows the master's transition from Historicism to Secessionism more clearly than all his other projects at the time. This stylistic change coincides with the beginning Wagner's professorial career at the Academy of Fine Arts (Page 42). It is possible that he was entrusted in April 1894, in his capacity as artistic advisor to the transport committee, with the design of the dam, together with a contract for the Stadtbahn (Page 84)(city rail system).

The dam, with its two almost six meter tall lion pylons (the bronze lions were created by the sculptor Rudolf Weyr) and the administration building compose a "City Waterway Gate." *"I always look forward to the two lions rising above the Danube on their bulwarks when I drive into town from the countryside. They are noble symbols of strength that*

NUSSDORFER WEHR-
UND SCHLEUSENANLAGE

Otto Wagner

have become landmarks... The combination of pure technical functionalism and the artist's sense of form created a new form of beauty that cannot be retrieved from the past" (Joseph August Lux).

The facility was re-fitted to meet the latest technical requirements in the seventies. The original needle dam was replaced with two sluicing gates. The new raised street built alongside during the renovation of the dam ruined the city gate effect completely.

STADTBAHN UND VORORTELINIE
Otto Wagner

I. – XXIII.

Sightseeing:
Open
to the public

Transportation:
Subways: U4, U6
City Rail

Otto Wagner built around 40 stops, 15 bridges, viaducts and an approximately 80-kilometer long track network (partially underground or under street level, with very few stations at street level). Wagner's network was meant for three transportation lines: the Stadtbahn (City Rail) line (from Heiligenstadt to Penzing), the Gürtel line (from Heiligenstadt to Meidlinger-Hauptstraße), the Wiental Donaukanal line (from Hütteldorf to Heiligenstadt via the main customs office) and the line to the 2nd district (from the main customs office to Praterstern).

Next to the Ringstraße, which was built in the 1860's, the Stadtbahn was the second visible and clearly recognizable connecting link in the Viennese cityscape. However, in contrast to the Ringstraße, the Stadtbahn connects the more recently developed city areas. Wagner integrated Vienna's suburbs and suburban areas in one large concentric circle with his project. He also understood the importance of planning breakthrough points and bridges with the radial streets in mind to avoid separating the inner from the outer city.

Wagner took the individual surroundings of each

station into consideration when designing them. In principle, there are two different types of station. Ground level supports were used to support the open tracks, which lie in the middle of two station halves. The underground stations are hall-like structures that create a form of track overpass. Wagner's inspiration for the Gürtel stations came from the gates to the city. Thus they acted as a reminder of the location's past – as part of the city's

1894
1901

I. – XXIII.

Sightseeing:
Open
to the public

Transportation:
Subways: U4, U6
City Rail

demarcation line and defensive wall. However, the outer form of the stations is a reference to the Vienna City gate par excellence, the outer Burgtor Gate erected between 1821–1824. It is completely white and bears the same circular and triglyph friezes as those on the stations.

The Karlsplatz station and Schönbrunn Pavilion for members of the imperial family and their guests are two exceptions in design terms. Wagner built the twin pavilions with the location of the Karlskirche constructed by Johann Bernhard Fischer von Erlach in mind. They were also influenced by the Secession exhibition hall built on the edge of Karlsplatz at the same time by Joseph Maria Olbrich. *"Both pavilions are masterpieces in their own way. The architect made them as small as permissible to allow for an undisturbed view of Karlskirche. The slender, light buildings are made of polished white marble and iron with Secession green décor. The walls are only 10 cm thick and consist of a merely two cm thick marble slab reinforced with five cm thick plaster panels separated by a three cm cavity. This facilitates heating the interior* (with the cash desk). *On the other hand, the exterior, with*

STADTBAHN UND VORORTELINIE

Otto Wagner

its imbedded gold ornaments can simply be washed when required, making it impervious to soot and dirt. The local reservations about blocking the view of the Karlskirche and so on soon faded away" (Ludwig Hevesi)

The court pavilion, built as a Baroque hunting temple, is slightly secluded and across the way from the Hietzing station in Schönbrunn. Inside, Wagner paid special attention to details, such as the rug of the Emperor's room, whose pattern shows the directions visitors should follow in this room, guiding them subconsciously.

SECESSION
Joseph Maria Olbrich

I.
Friedrichstraße 12

Sightseeing:
Open
to the public

Transportation:
Subways: U1, U2,
U4 (Karlsplatz)

In 1897, a number of Viennese artists left the Vienna Künstlerhaus due to their dissatisfaction with the respected hall's exhibition policies. Following the example of the Munich Secession, the Viennese artists founded the Vienna Secession. These artists considered it their duty to summarize all new, avant-garde currents in order to present them to a broader segment of the population.

Joseph Maria Olbrich, a close associate of Otto Wagner's, was chosen to complete construction on the project. Gustav Klimt, one of the young artist association's leading members and the author of a sketch for the building influenced Olbrich's original flamboyant design. The building was initially planned as a temporary structure and was constructed on eight-meter deep cement columns that reached down to the Ottakring Creek underneath the hall. Olbrich completed the task by distributing the structure's volume between the representative frontispiece and the simple exhibition hall. Room space could be adjusted with movable separation walls to meet the respective needs.

The slogan above the door "Der Zeit ihre Kunst, der Kunst ihre Freiheit" (Arts for the time, freedom for the arts) came from the art critic Ludwig Hevesi. Ernst Klimt, Gustav's brother, designed the bronze doors of the entrance. The lateral mosaic vases borne by bronze turtles designed by Robert Örley were put up a few years later.

The Viennese were never at a loss for a nickname and called the building with its striking bronze leaf cupola the "cabbage head" or the "Assyrian water closet" because of its large white walls and cubist appearance.

The hall was renovated and redesigned on the inside by Adolf Krischanitz between 1982 and 1986.

WIENZEILEHÄUSER
Otto Wagner

VI.
Linke Wienzeile 40,
Linke Wienzeile 38,
Köstlergasse 1,
Köstlergasse 3

Sightseeing:
none

Transportation:
Subway: U4
(Kettenbrücken-
gasse)

The three apartment and business projects on the Wienzeile represent another case in which Otto Wagner assumed both contracting and architectural responsibilities. This was the case with almost all of his larger urban apartment house projects and it gave him almost complete creative control, allowing him to realize his vision almost entirely. These buildings mark the architect's departure from Historicism and dedication to the birth of a new style. The impetus of this stylistic transition would have been unthinkable without the cooperation of Wagner's younger associates and pupils (Joseph Maria Olbrich, Josef Plečnik, Hubert Gessner and others).

Despite the differing facades and structural details, the buildings are recognizable as a cohesive ensemble that achieves its effect due to the unique urban corner location. The building at Wienzeile 40 is completely covered with colorful stoneware tiles. This explains the building's nickname, "Majolica House". The stone paneling was representative of Wagner's theory on the unification of practical, useful features with aesthetic elements. For Wagner,

WIENZEILEHÄUSER

Otto Wagner

the great advantage of such a facade design was the fact that it was almost indestructible and looked like new after a simple wash.

In constructing the building at the particularly prominent urban location on the corner of Wienzeile 38 / Köstlergasse 1, the architect concentrated on the architectural plasticity of the corner solution. The main facade of the building facing the Wienzeile was elaborately decorated with gold-plated relieved medallions designed by Kolo Moser. Othmar Schimkowitz created the "calling damsel" statues. The other two buildings feature plaster façades and reliefs. The building at Köstlergasse 3, was the site of Otto Wagner's "quarters", which also contained his lost glass bathtub.

GLASHAUS BURGGARTEN

Friedrich Ohmann, Ludwig Baumann

1899–1905
1910–1911

I.
Burggarten

Sightseeing:
Partially open to
the public, see
opening hours

Transportation:
Streetcar lines:
1, 2, D, J,
Subway: U2.
Bus: 3A
(Oper)

The Burggarten glasshouse is one of the last art-
fully designed examples of this popular 19th century building type. Shortly after Friedrich Ohmann
was called from Prague to Vienna in 1899 to assume
the supervision of construction at the Neue Hofburg (Page 56), the Comptroller of the Imperial
Household appointed him to build a, "new winter
garden" to replace the old "Glashaus im Kaiser-
garten" built between 1823 and 1826.

The glasshouse's central portal structure is emphasized by the monumental columns positioned before
the two lower wings. These end in stone corner
pavilions with tent roofs. The richly plastic, partly
late Historicist, partly Secessionist ornaments were
designed by the sculptors Edmund Hellmer, Josef
Václav Myslbek and Rudolf Weyr.

In 1910/11, Ohmann's successor as head of construction at the Hofburg, Ludwig Baumann, built
the second heated wing and the Albrechtstor, a
gate which gives visitors access to the park from
Hanuschgasse.

Although the building is not a pioneering struc-

GLASHAUS BURGGARTEN

Friedrich Ohmann, Ludwig Baumann

1899–1905
1910–1911

ture in terms of construction or style, its integration between the Late Historicist new Hofburg, the High Baroque National Library and the Classicist Albertinapalais (the Albertina was given a Historicist façade around 1860) remains a remarkable feat.

The massive stone walls were Ohmann's reaction to the new Hofburg. The copper tent roofs continue the National Library motif and the low lateral wings allowed for an unrestricted view of the Albertina. The incorporation of modern building techniques enabled Ohmann to create a striking combination of the two main styles of his time: Baroque and Jugendstil architecture.

WOHN- UND GESCHÄFTSHAUS
PORTOIS & FIX

Max Fabiani

III.
Ungargasse 59–61

Sightseeing:
Open
in the shops

Transportation:
Streetcar line: O
(Neulinggasse)

Max Fabiani was the pupil of Carl König, a conservative professor at the Vienna Technical University and an employee at Otto Wagner's studio from 1894 until 1898. With the apartment and commercial building he constructed for the Portois & Fix furniture company, Fabiani not only cited but attempted to surpass the example set by Wagner with the facade of the Majolica House on Linke Wienzeile (Page 80). Fabiani's facade design goes beyond Wagner's attempt to unite practical, useful elements with aesthetic features.

The difference made by progress between the stone panels on the Majolica House and the Portois & Fix building lies in the fact that the sumptuous Jugendstil floral decor is not related to the structure of the stone panels. Fabiani, on the other hand, uses the pattern of the pyrolitic granite tiles (from the ceramics workshop in Szolnay, Fünfkirchen) by combining the different green toned panels to create slender and delicate, but also strictly geometrical ornaments that integrate the floor and axis of the facade. *"Every detail on the façade is*

primarily functional and only decorative as such."
(Marco Pozzetto)

This smooth surface is sparingly embellished and contrasts with the relieved metal décor: the metal window frames create the illusion of drawn curtains. The plaster finish visible on the base course of the building today was the result of poor restoration work, this part of the structure originally featured Swedish granite tiles.

Behind the street side of the building lie the extensive furniture factory facilities that spread almost to Dannebergplatz.

WOHNHAUS BECKGASSE (VILLA LANGER)
Josef Plečnik

XIII.
Beckgasse 30

Sightseeing:
None

Transportation:
Streetcar line: 60
(Gloriettegasse)

Josef Plečnik was both one of the first and the most original of Otto Wagner's pupils. He only got involved in the construction of his first project, a residential building for the contractor Karl Beck relatively late. By the time Plečnik joined the effort, the building's foundations had already been laid. He was only able to influence the facade design significantly. Plečnik had prefabricated ornaments mass-produced and set in the plaster at regular intervals. *"It isn't possible to formulate the division between structure and ornament forms with greater clarity"* (August Sarnitz). The division is defined by the fact that the inner room structure is expressed with large, partly convex windows on the outside of the building. In contrast to this, the facade's relieved ornaments consisting of rose-buds and wavy lines is consciously non-tectonic. The brick-lined edge of the kitchen window was given a humorous note with a fully articulated goose head on the upper level. Plečnik followed the example of Hector Guimard's Castel Béranger

WOHNHAUS BECKGASSE (VILLA LANGER)
Josef Plečnik

with the animal sculpture, but the influence of Belgian Art Nouveau (Victor Horta) and the Viennese modern architecture of the period (Joseph Maria Olbrich and Otto Wagner) are also undeniable.

After construction was completed, Josef Plečnik said with a tone of resignation: *"In any case, the program had already been conceived stupidly in the contractor's imagination, making any healthy result impossible. But I wanted to be exceptional and that was the right decision. I will never progress if I don't take my chances while I am young."*

ARTARIA-HAUS
Max Fabiani

1.
Kohlmarkt 9

Sightseeing:
Only in the shops

Transportation:
Subways: U1, U3
(Stephansplatz)

The Artaria publishing house building is slightly recessed from the other buildings, giving it a narrow forecourt. Its daring façade design creates the impression of *"heralding the 'impending disaster' ... in the form of Loos' Michaelerhaus* (Page 146) *... in its immediate vicinity."* (August Sarnitz)
The division of the building into a commercial and residential part can be seen clearly in the façade

ARTARIA-HAUS

Max Fabiani

design. The two base course levels were built primarily in glass and are joined by four red marble pillars and completed with a visible iron traverse at the top. The pillars carry the stories above both visually and structurally, with two sculptures by Alfonso Canciani located in front of the columns. The façade segment of the four higher stories is fitted with white marble slabs in keeping with Wagner's Majolica house (Page 80).

Another remarkable feature is the egalitarian design of the four main stories, which are only separated by narrow cornices under the window ledges. Fabiani used bay windows for the first time in Vienna on this project. This British design was used very frequently in Vienna over the next few years. The house was completed with a wreath-shaped cornice including a coffered ornament underneath that was inspired by the Wagner school and reflects the small forecourt in front on the sidewalk. It is placed diagonally on the building over a wide egg-shaped capital.

The entrance to the building on this difficult plot of land was set in a deep hallway at the side of the house. An oval staircase leads up to the floors of the building.

DOPPELWOHNHAUS MOSER-MOLL I
Josef Hoffmann

XIX.
Steinfeldgasse 6–8
Geweygasse 13

Sightseeing:
None

Transportation:
Streetcar line: 37
(Geweygasse)

Josef Hoffmann started his architecture studies under Carl von Hasenauer and completed them under Otto Wagner. He cited English country style architecture in building the twin apartment buildings for the artistic entrepreneur Kolo Moser and the painter Carl Moll. The hipped roof and latticed gable created a strong link to country style design that is atypical for prototypical twin urban apartment buildings. This was Hoffman's reaction to the conflicting topography of the building's location at the edge of the Viennese villa district.

The two linked buildings create a visual unit, giving them the appearance of a single building. Only the interiors make it clear that Haus Moll is considerably larger than Haus Moser. Both buildings are laid out around a central staircase.

Another of the architect's goals was to integrate the building and its decor in one unit. *"... a house whose interior is already revealed on the exterior."* (Josef Hoffmann) In order to achieve this, the architect created the impression of movement in modeling the building and paid special attention to the structure's spatial sequence and formal details.

DOPPELWOHNHAUS MOSER-MOLL I
Josef Hoffmann

The surface colors and textures also played an important roll in these efforts.

The twin Moser-Moll buildings create a complete ensemble together with the villas Hoffman built shortly thereafter for Hugo Henneberg and Friedrich Spitzer (Page 98).

ENGEL-APOTHEKE

Oskar Laske

I.
Bognergasse 9

Sightseeing:
During opening
hours

Transportation:
Subways: U1, U3
(Stephansplatz)

Oskar Laske, a pupil of Otto Wagner's, who later
dedicated himself exclusively to his painting, was
hired to build an apartment building featuring a
store on the narrow plot of land. The house's layout is unremarkable, with a narrow winding staircase leading to the top levels. The façade, on the
other hand, shows Laske's desire to apply Wagner's
teachings.
The rich floral decoration of the portal of the

ENGEL-APOTHEKE

Oskar Laske

1901
1902

Engel-Apotheke extending over the two lower levels contrasts with the stringently geometric structure of the building. This was a successful (to this day) attempt to attract the attention of passersby.

The glass mosaic shows two angels on stone pedestals raising healing potions with the snake of aesculapius creeping up their arms in correspondence with the name and purpose of the store. The head of each figure bears a gold-plated ringlet. A sunflower frieze was also imbedded in the wall above the large rectangular top level window, which is decorated with a wrought iron bars and a leaf frieze. As opposed to the exterior portal design, the original interior décor still follows Late Historicist teachings.

The portal zone is considered one of the most decorative examples of the use of "pure" Secessionist style elements (Page 78) in Viennese architecture. At the same time, it is one of the few remaining undiluted examples of a style that is so popular all over the world today.

DOPPELMIETHAUS STEGGASSE
Josef Plečnik

V.
Rechte
Wienzeile 68
Steggasse I
Hamburgerstraße 16

Sightseeing:
None

Transportation:
Subway: U4
(Kettenbrücken-
gasse)

The urban planning requirements dictated by the River Wien, the sloping Steggasse and the slightly curved trajectory of Hamburgerstrasse in this area forced Plečnik to build and apply decorations carefully. The difference in height of the two structures is a reaction to the sloping terrain. It also helps define the project as two residential units. The freestanding building is structured by its details. The dominating wreath-shaped cornice and the (glass-floored) balconies leading around the corner of the building accentuate the double cor-

DOPPELMIETHAUS STEGGASSE
Josef Plečnik

1901
1902

ner location, which Plečnik emphasized even further with a double turn. The architect emulated his
master Otto Wagner's work on the corner apartment house at Linke Wienzeile 38 / Köstlergasse 1
(Page 81) by using varying amounts of decor on
the building. Plečnik applied greater amounts of
plaster decor to the visible side of the building
facing the River Wien. The architect countered
the danger of giving the facades a rigid appearance
by applying Lisene edging along the entire height
of the building to give it a more youthful appearance.

Plečnik also incorporated the example of Wagner's
"Hosenträgerhaus" on Universitätsstraße (Page 64)
and American elements such as those of the
Chicago School.

The building contractor was once again– as in the
case of the single family house on Beckgasse (Page
86) – Carl Langer, the city building contractor. The
goose sculpture next to the window on Beckgasse
was an expression of Plečnik's humor and the sati-
rical inscription on the sills of the mezzanine windows that read "Greislerei mit Architekturartikel
des Jos. Plecnius pisoul."

VILLA VOJCSIK
Otto Schönthal

XIV.
Linzer Straße 375

Sightseeing:
None

Transportation:
Streetcar line: 49
(Bahnhofstraße)

The Villa Vojcsik contract, which was for an apartment building and medical practice, was awarded to the then only 22 year-old Otto Schönthal on the recommendation of his teacher, Otto Wagner. Ladislaus Vojcsik was Wagner's private physician, with whom he regularly played tarot (at times, Wagner resided close to Villa Vojcsik in his villa at Hüttelbergstraße 26). Although the house is located in a close row of houses in a typical Viennese suburban area, Schönthal was able to give the house a freestanding air by elevating the middle section and linking the lower lateral pediments to the neighboring buildings. The four-axle central wing features a striking canopy roof while the one-axle lateral pediments appear to lack roofs. The placement of the windows along the roof crest make them similar to those used by Josef Hoffmann on the Palais Stoclet in Brussels at the same time.

The unusual lateral pediment openings on the ground level result from the overlapping semi-circular arches and the angular wall pillars. The ornaments made of cubist metal structures, poly-

Otto Schönthal

chrome, relieved tiles, laurel wreaths and festoons complete the building's unique appearance. The garden-side façade is even more cleverly designed and features more plastics.

This villa is one of the rare actually-completed examples of the more daring Wagner School designs built around 1900. The flat wood and cement roof shows that Schönthal was also influenced by the Mediterranean tradition – as were other Wagner pupils. The building was thoroughly renovated by the architect Boris Podrecca between 1975 and 1982.

WOHNHAUS SPITZER

Josef Hoffmann

Sightseeing:
None

Transportation:
Streetcar line: 37
(Hohe Warte)

Together with the twin Moser-Moll building (Page 90) and Haus Henneberg, Haus Spitzer composes an ensemble of early buildings in the "Villenkolonie Hohe Warte," which was later expanded. Joseph Maria Olbrich had won the competition for this project, but Josef Hoffman took over when Olbrich departed for Darmstadt, Germany. The emphatically structured building is dominated by the British Arts and Crafts Movement elements. The projecting entrance, featuring a flat roof that doubles as a terrace, gives the building an additional sense of liveliness. The contractor Dr. Friedrich Spitzer, who was a passionate, internationally acclaimed amateur photographer, kept his studio in the room with bay windows on the ground floor. The versatile Dr. Spitzer was born in

WOHNHAUS SPITZER
Josef Hoffmann

Brno and grew up in Zurich. He was a member of the "Camera-Club" and worked with the photographer Hugo Henneberg, another Hoffman contractor.

The house also contained a room decorated by Olbrich, "The Blue Room", which he had designed for Spitzer's earlier apartment on Schleifmühlgasse. *"And in Dr. Spitzer's house, where I dropped anchor in one of Hoffman's square, high-back chairs, I looked at Spitzer's blue room. It brings the first Secessionist period to mind, when they reached out for all the colorful stars in the sky in order to hammer them into this earth's tent."* (Ludwig Hevesi)

Robert Örley

1902

The "Zum schwarzen Kameel" delicatessen and restaurant was founded as a spice-trading store by Johann Baptist Cameel in 1618. According to a popular tale, the camellia bears the name of a Cameel family member. At the beginning of the 19th century, the store was expanded to include a wine tavern, which was often frequented by Ludwig van Beethoven. Lord Nelson and Lady Hamilton also visited the locale during their stay in Vienna in 1800.

In 1898, Franz Josef Alois Stiebitz, the owner of the "k. u. k. Hof-Specereiwaren- und Weinhandlung" (Imperial and Royal Spice and Wine Merchants) hired Joseph Urban to draft preliminary plans for a new building. However, the old building was only torn down in 1901. Although Julius Mayreder had been a founding member of the Secession (Page 78) in 1897, Mayreder, the brother-in-law of the

I.
Bognergasse 5

Sightseeing:
None

Transportation:
Subways: U1, U2
(Stephansplatz)

RESTAURATION "ZUM SCHWARZEN KAMEEL"

Robert Örley

writer Rosa Mayreder, constructed the building as a Late Historicist, classicist structure. A stucco frieze in the bar area bears the name of the contractor and the date the building was completed.

Robert Örley, who trained as a carpenter before studying architecture created the locale's remarkable décor, which is still intact today. He had already discussed contemporary furniture in two essays three years before and defended Adolf Loos' Café Museum built in 1899. He acted in accordance with his own theoretical considerations and the modern principles of the arts and crafts trade. He designed every furniture piece to suit its purpose in the sales and bar area, and yet succeeded in creating one harmonic unit within. His use of oak wood intarsia applications and tiles represents a departure from Adolf Loos' design principles.

WOHN- UND GESCHÄFTSHAUS "RÜDIGER-HOF"

Oskar Marmorek

The "Rüdiger-Hof" – named after Rüdigergasse – is one building in an ensemble of high-quality apartment buildings on Hamburgerstraße constructed around 1900. Due to the fact that the "Rüdiger-Hof" is a mostly visible, three-front structure on one of Vienna's most important city access routes, it is of particular urban architectural importance within the ensemble. The architect Oskar Marmorek had studied under Carl König at the Vienna Technical University and earned his reputation as the designer of large amusement parks ("Venice in Vienna", Prater 1895) and exhibition parks (replica of the Ofen Royal Castle at the millennium exhibition in Budapest, 1896). Marmorek is one of the few Viennese architects who successfully completed a number projects in Budapest. Along with Theodor Herzl, he was also one of the founders of the Zionist Movement.

A projecting roof crowned with metal décor covers the flat central structure of the cube-shaped building. It is possible that the site's location on the banks of the River Wien inspired Marmorek to use the striking waved-shaped décor in the ground level area. A laurel tree frieze decoration was planned for the uppermost levels. This idea was ultimately realized as an abstract, almost purely geometric pattern on the finished builder. The upper levels each contain two large apartments. The coffee house on the ground level containing a reading room, billiard-room and somewhat higher gaming-room, still features the original wall paneling and furniture today. The original vibrant coloring of the building was restored during an extensive renovation completed in 1992.

V.
Hamburgerstraße 20

Sightseeing:
None

Transportation:
Subway: U4
(Pilgramgasse)

WOHN- UND GESCHÄFTSHAUS
"RÜDIGER-HOF"
Oskar Marmorek

1902

HOHE BRÜCKE
Josef Hackhofer

I.
Wipplingerstraße
Tiefer Graben

Sightseeing:
Open
to the public

Transportation:
Subway: U2
(Schottentor)

The bridge over Tiefer Graben between the two buildings on Wipplingerstrasse 21 and 22 goes back to Roman times and the Babenberger period. In its earlier form, the bridge spanned the Ottakring Creek that flowed down Tiefer Graben in front of the gates of the city. The bridge over the 15-meter gap of Tiefer Graben on Wipplinger-straße was first referred to as the "Hohe Brücke" in 1295. A pointed stone arch supported by two mighty walls was added in the 15th century and stone steps leading down Tiefer Graben were built later.

The aging bridge was replaced with a Neo-Gothic structure in 1857/58, when Wipplingerstraße was widened. This structure was in turn torn down in 1903, after cracks were detected in it. Together with the structural engineer Karl Christl and the iron construction specialist Anton Biró, the Carinthian architect and bridge builder Josef Hackhofer created a Jugendstil bridge, the new

HOHE BRÜCKE
Josef Hackhofer

1904

"Hohe Brücke." Hackhofer, who had built a number of bridges in cooperation with Friedrich Ohmann, Otto Wagner and others, made clever use of the spectacular location. He used a complete paneling technique to emphasize the bridge's architecture. Seen from Wipplingerstrasse, the sumptuous Jugendstil decorations on the railing and candelabras give the structure the appearance of a bridge. When viewed from Tiefen Graben, it seems to be a round arch of a gate (with built-in showcases in the supports). He also made use of Baroque staircases down to Tiefer Graben.

The narrow ends of the marble slabs feature renditions of the bridges that stood there before. The wrought iron skeleton of the bridge is reminiscent of the Stadtbahn pavilions Otto Wagner had previously built on Karlsplatz (Page 76).

I.
Stadtpark

Sightseeing:
Open
to the public

Transportation:
Subway: U4
(Stadtpark)

In 1898, Friedrich Ohmann, who was a professor at the Academy of Fine Arts and the architect of the new Hofburg (Page 56) at the time, was commissioned by the City of Vienna's Water Board to adapt all buildings and bridges affected by the flow of the River Wien. This led to the construction of the River Wien Administration building in Hadersdorf-Weidlingau and the Hietzing and Schönbrunn bridges. He planned a large romantic and dreamy portal for the opening at the end of the park where the river flowed freely. He constructed Baroque-Impressionist bank walls, terraces, promenades, steps and pavilions that are not devoid of Jugendstil elements. This is contrary to the design of his colleague Otto Wagner's Stadtbahn

WIENFLUSSVERBAUUNG IM STADTPARK
Friedrich Ohmann

station nearby, which was built in a Secessionist style. (Page 78). His plan compensated cleverly for the shift of the river's axis away from the Lothringerstraße axis, which was an unaesthetic feature of the river. The picturesque park offers a unique experience and is harmoniously linked to the older park segment.

Ohmann was forced to leave the complex unfinished. Grotesque animal sculptures, including crocodiles or water-spewing elephants and a grotto featuring a waterfall as protection against the "foul smelling hole," were not completed. Ohmann also built the Trinkhalle (a small bistro Meierei) in the Stadtpark. The City Gardens Administration building was built according to plans by Josef Bittner.

In 1985–87, the architect Hermann Czech replaced the old wooden walkway over the River Wien with a new pedestrian bridge.

ZACHERLHAUS

Josef Plečnik

I.
Brandstätte 6
Wildpretmarkt 2–4

Sightseeing:
None

Transportation:
Subway: U1, U3
(Stephansplatz)

Josef Plečnik won the competition limited to Otto Wagner's pupils for this project in 1900, but the final plans were only drafted in 1903.

The three-front building, which the writer Peter Altenberg also wrote about, is one of the most important early examples of Wagner School architecture. A structurally demanding variation of the "paneling" theme both Wagner and his pupils pursued time and again (Majolikahaus) (Page 80), (Postsparkasse) (Page 110), (Portois & Fix by Max Fabiani) (Page 84) was employed here. The architect mounted gray-brown slabs of granite in irregularly spaced and fixed grooves, giving the façade structure its own unique rhythm. Behind it lies a tight grid of ferroconcrete struts, which compose the structural skeleton of the building.

ZACHERLHAUS
Josef Plečnik

1903
1905

Plečnik compensated for the disadvantageous shape of the site with an impressive architectural feat. The powerful rounded front of the building, facing Brandstätte, was compared to a chestnut oven in contemporary caricatures. The statue of the Archangel Michael made of hammered copper was nicknamed the *"The Flea Slayer"* with the approval of the contractor – the moth insecticide producer Johann Evangelist Zacherl. Franz Metzner created the majolica atlas figures on the top level, which compose a wreath-shaped cornice in combination with the curved windows.

The interior contrasts starkly with the long, dark foyer and the elegant boat-shaped staircase. Curiously, some of the lamps are shaped like insects.

POSTSPARKASSE
Otto Wagner

I.
Georg-Coch-Platz 2

Sightseeing:
Erdgeschoß,
Kassenhalle

Transportation:
Streetcar lines: 1, 2,
Subway: U3
(Stubentor)

Planning for the Postsparkasse began in the 1890's, when it became necessary to solve construction problems in the Stubenring area. To everybody's surprise, including the architect's, Otto Wagner won the competition in 1903 although his proposal did not match competition requirements. Perfect symmetry was Wagner's guiding principle when he designed the five-point layout plan. The plan featured a glass-covered hall for the teller area. Joseph August Lux, Otto Wagner's biographer, found words of description for the building that are still accurate today: *"Nothing about the Postsparkasse reminds us of 'free Renaissance Style'. No*

POSTSPARKASSE
Otto Wagner

reminiscence of historical styles, no Palazzo architecture, no monumentality taken from architectural history. Instead, everything is functional. The materials used command attention. Ferroconcrete, glass, aluminum, hard rubber, etc., those are the materials this building is made of. All of them are new! No architect would have considered this possible when the Länderbank was built. Otto Wagner discovered them. He may not have invented these materials, but he did give them their current importance, discovered their functional architectural application."

The stone façade paneling is stressed with over-dimensional visible bolts. The poetic-rational design continues on the inside. The technical construction theme of the teller area with its glass floor and suspended steel-glass structure nonetheless satisfies aesthetic demands and proved to be a lasting influence on 20th century architecture.

KAISERIN-ELISABETH-DENKMAL
Friedrich Ohmann

I.
Volksgarten

Sightseeing:
Open
to the public

Transportation:
Streetcar lines: 1, 2,
D, (Burgtheater),
Subway: U3
(Herrengasse)

The monument to the empress, who was murde-
red in 1898, was the result of a citizen's collection
initiative among the population. After much debate, a site close to Löwelstraße in the Volksgarten
was chosen, and the project competition was
announced, calling Austrian artists to submit proposals. The jury decided that none of the 67 designs that were submitted was adequate. Without
having participated in the competition, Friedrich
Ohmann, the architect of the new Hofburg (Page
56), sent in a sketch that showed the empress sit-
ting on a garden bench. This idea was used as the
basis for a second, more selective competition in
1903. The model submitted in Hans Bitterlichs' and
Ohmann's architectural design won this second
round.

The memorial attempts to capture the atmosphere
of Greece, the empress's favorite country. At the
same time, Ohmann cites Christian religious building in his layout. The long paths on each side

KAISERIN-ELISABETH-DENKMAL

Friedrich Ohmann

remind the visitor of a church choir aisle. Instead of using a four-way intersection, Ohmann built a pond and finally placed the sculpture of the seated empress on a semi-circular apse rather than on an altar. The numerous depictions of roses are based on a festive poem in which the empress was referred to as the *"Bavarian rose"* on her arrival in Vienna.

The monument wasn't only intended as a memorial to the empress that would strengthen the link between the monarchy and the population. It was supposed to once again strengthen Austro-Hungarian ties after they were weakened by the talks held in 1867, the empress having great affection for Hungary.

KARL-BORROMÄUS-BRUNNEN
(LUEGER-BRUNNEN)

Josef Engelhart, Josef Plečnik

III.
Karl-Borromäus-
Platz

Sightseeing:
Open
to the public

Transportation:
Subway: U3
(Rochusgasse)

The fountain was built and named in honor of the popular Viennese mayor Dr. Karl Lueger (1844-1910). After the Zauberflötenbrunnen (Magic Flute Fountain) that was built around the same time on Mozartplatz (Page 120), it was the second significant Secessionist fountain built in Vienna. In 1904, Richard Kauffungen built another fountain on Siebenbrunnenplatz, in Vienna's 5th district.
A three-sided obelisk lies at the center of the fountain with three lions' mouths at its feet. Water pours into a multi-tub bronze pool mounted on cherubs. Three groups of figures are depicted showing the deeds of St. Karl Borromäus (St. Karl Borromäus healing a sick noble woman and a mother and

KARL-BORROMÄUS-BRUNNEN
(LUEGER-BRUNNEN)
Josef Engelhart, Josef Plečnik

child, the healing of maladies and the plague in Milan).

Engelhart wrote the following on integrating the fountain in the limited space that was available: *"Since the new project contained fifteen larger than life figures of children, two different horizons had to be created in order to accommodate the differing scales. Thus the basin had to be recessed in the ground. The oval fountain walls were chosen because of the plot's irregularity, since it would have been difficult to fit a perfect square into the space. This helped give the monument its own personal character."*

The painter and sculptor Josef Engelhart consulted with Josef Plenik only when construction was already underway. The first stone was set on October 24th, 1904, Mayor Karl Lueger's birthday. The fountain was renovated in 1949, after having been damaged during WWII.

SANATORIUM PURKERSDORF

Josef Hoffmann

Purkersdorf
Wiener Straße 74

Sightseeing:
None

Transportation:
Westbahn
(Purkersdorf)

After being commissioned by the Director Viktor Zuckerkandl, the brother-in-law of the well-known art critic Berta Zuckerkandl, Josef Hoffmann planned the "Sanatorium Westend" as a rest home offering baths and physical therapy. Although it is located right on Vienna's city limits, it is Hoffman's main Viennese project. It is also one of the most important examples of 19th century architecture.

"It is the first modern solution that addresses long hidden and nurtured ideas. Hoffmann's layout gives full consideration and organization to the needs of a sanatorium. He remembers the experience and beauty of simple forms and lets every building approach the other with clear words. He avoids using any form of splendor or ornamentation. The entrance is emphasized only by two friezes. The walls are smooth and lightly colored inside and outside and the windows lack frames and ledges. The roof slightly projects outward slightly and is flat. The white furniture heightens the impression of hygienic cleanliness". (L. W. Rochowanski)

Hoffmann made the ferroconcrete structure partly visible on the inside. In keeping with his concept of creating a complete work of art, Hoffman called on the Wiener Werkstätte, of which he was the

SANATORIUM PURKERSDORF
Josef Hoffmann

director, to design the interiors. Black and white contrasts are the dominant element at the Sanatorium Purkersdorf, though Hoffman built the Palais Stoclet in Brussels shortly thereafter with emphatically colorful interiors, creating a unique symbiosis of the fine arts. The sanatorium furniture belongs to the most important examples of this art in the 20th century.

The elements added to the building by Leopold Bauer in 1926 against Hoffman's will disfigured the structure. They were removed in 1995 as part of the exterior renovation.

KIRCHE AM STEINHOF
Otto Wagner

XIV.
Baumgartner
Höhe I

Sightseeing:
During opening
hours

Transportation:
Streetcar line: 46,
Bus: 48A
(Psychiatrisches
Krankenhaus)

The ground plans created by Otto Wagner served as the basis for the construction of the Lower Austrian Hospital and Rest Home, today's "Am Steinhof" Psychiatric Clinic. Wagner drafted the plans for a competition to build the facility's church that his two pupils Leopold Bauer and Otto Schönthal had entered. Wagner was only awarded a contract to build the church for the patron saint of Lower Austria, Saint Leopold, and he built it at the highest point of the hierarchically structured pavilion grounds.

The building gave Wagner the chance to realize his vision of "modern church building" and "architecture for our time." Based on the traditional layout of a Greek cross, the building is crowned with a high cupola calculated to be clearly visible at a distance. The façade features thin marble paneling and the interior is light, offering an unimpaired view of the altar.

Hygiene, cleanliness and the fact that the church was for a clinic were Wagner's guiding design principles. He created soap dispenser type holy water fountains to prevent infection. The church floor

KIRCHE AM STEINHOF
Otto Wagner

1907

slopes down towards the altar to facilitate cleaning
and he furnished the church with extremely short
benches for attendants to be able to quickly inter-
vene if a patient suffered a seizure.

Despite all these practical details, Wagner never
lost sight of the aesthetic aspects of this church
project, in contradiction to his maxim: *"Something
that is impractical can never be beautiful."*
A contemporary critic likened the Christian
church to the, "tomb of an Indian Maharaja."

ZAUBERFLÖTENBRUNNEN (MOZARTBRUNNEN)
Carl Wollek, Otto Schönthal

IV.
Mozartplatz

Sightseeing:
Open
to the public

Transportation:
Subway: U1
(Taubstummen-
gasse)

The fountain was built only after 29 proposals were submitted in a competition won by Künstlerhaus member Carl Wollek against the Secessionist Richard Luksch. The site's architecture was designed by Otto Schönthal, a pupil of Otto Wagner. The fountain's sculpture by Wollek depicts the key scene in the last act between the two main characters in Mozart's "The Magic Flute." On the occasion of the fountain's inauguration, the October 8th 1905 issue of the Neues Wiener Tagblatt described Wollek's design as, *"Tamino and Pamina, two youthful, slender figures nestling closely together, walk through the water. Tamino's magical flute playing defeats the ghosts of the deep (represented by two hideous heads) who resist in vain and are then banished and defeated. This group is set simply and clearly on a substructure consisting of four fish heads who spray slender jets of water into a flat, oval basin. The back bears the dedication and two drainage openings. The figures are made of bronze and the basin and superstructure are made of hardened sandstone."*
The fountain was meant to be the main focus on Wiedner Hauptstraße. Mozart's opera was perfor-

ZAUBERFLÖTENBRUNNEN (MOZARTBRUNNEN)

Carl Wollek, Otto Schönthal

1905

med for the first time on September 30th, 1791 at the Freihaustheater located close by.

Although Wollek was not a member of the Secession (Page 78), the monument, which was inaugurated on October 8th, 1905, is nonetheless one of the most important public Secessionist sculptures.

In 1927, Wollek designed a second Mozart Fountain in St. Gilgen / Salzburg.

SCHNEIDERSALON KNIŽE
Adolf Loos

I.
Graben 13

Sightseeing:
During opening hours

Transportation:
Subways: U1, U3
(Stephansplatz)

The Kniže tailoring salon is the oldest preserved example of Adolf Loos' work in Vienna. Loos applied sales psychology to the narrow portal design. *"The lateral granite columns of the massive frame guide you to the showcases and entrance via an s-shaped curve. However, the base course doesn't follow this movement, which keeps passersby at a certain distance from the large front showcases. Whoever wants to inspect the merchandise more closely has to move in and enter the*

SCHNEIDERSALON KNIŽE

Adolf Loos

1905
1913

narrow space between the showcases, which almost places him directly in the store. This is the trick behind such a threshold that it is crossed without the perhaps potential customer noticing." (Otto Kapfinger) The small showcases on the concave-convex walls of the portal that swing in towards the store were added later.

The black granite portal and the narrow cherry wood sales room on the ground floor do not hint at the generous row of high-ceilinged presentation rooms on the upper level that can be reached via the simple spiral steps. Loos, who considered British gentlemen's tailoring the only true form of fashion, gave these rooms the atmosphere of a fine London gentlemen's club. Or, as Friedrich Achleitner wrote, *"(Of) an ocean liners' first class salon."* They are made with matching oak wood panels. The inward-projecting galleries are also used by the workshop on the third floor.

Overall, the elegant store is a successful balancing act between public presentation and refined privacy.

In following years, Loos went on to design the Kniže stores in Prague, Berlin and Paris as well. The Viennese store was expanded by Italian architect Paolo Piva in 1993.

SCHÜTZENHAUS
Otto Wagner

1906
1908

II.
Obere
Donaustraße 26

Sightseeing:
None

Transportation:
Streetcar lines: 1, 2,
(Schottentor)

It was necessary to build the Schützenhaus (flood-gate house) at the "Kaiserbad Barrage Facility" (it was meant to replace the old "Kaiserbad", one of many bathing sites built along the Danube Canal) in order to convert the Danube Canal into a trade and winter port. Otto Wagner was hired as artistic consultant to the traffic commission – as he had been a few years back on the Nuss-dorf dam – and asked to draft plans. The two additional sluicing gates and dams that would have been necessary to complete the conversion were not built.

The blue-white tiles and the subtle wavy lines that reflect the river give this building its striking, site-specific functionalist appearance. *"The main dimensions of the building were defined by the tasks the structure has to fulfill. It is supposed to offer a protective shell for the steel frame structures of the*

SCHÜTZENHAUS
Otto Wagner

mechanical lifting devices, storage space for shooting targets and finally, enough space for the required administration." (Wiener Bauindustrie-Zeitung, 1910)

The ground floor of the building was largely used as the floodgate storage room. A fixed dam crane was located on the upper level, as well as quarters for the dam watchman. The crane could be used to move a dam structure that was embedded in the river. A second, movable crane was then used to set the floodgate section of the structure. The original function of the house can be recognized clearly due to the projecting cranes. The glass dam crane cockpit on the upper floor is still intact, but the building became obsolete when the dam was removed many years ago.

NEUE WIENER HANDELSAKADEMIE

Julius and Wunibald Deininger

1906
1908

VIII.
Hamerlingplatz 5–6
Schönborn-
gasse 3–5

Sightseeing:
By appointment

Transportation:
Streetcar lines: 5, 33,
J, (Albertgasse)

The school building is located on a plot of land between Hamerlingplatz and Schönborngasse and features a main wing, two lateral wings, two symmetrical staircases and a centrally located ceremonial hall. The structure is product of a father-son collaboration between Julius and Wunibald Deininger. *"One has the impression that this is a particularly pleasing example of cooperation between two generations of architects. It seems Julius, the experienced father, offered his impetuous son, who had just grown out of the Wagner School, the right framework of help and counterbalancing advice."* (Friedrich Achleitner)

NEUE WIENER HANDELSAKADEMIE
Julius and Wunibald Deininger

The imposing main front of the building faces the large expanse of Hamerlingplatz, while the façade facing Schönborngasse is much less sophisticated. Wunibald Deininger is considered one of Otto Wagner's most gifted pupils and it can be assumed that he was responsible for the design of the main façade on Hamerlingplatz. He designed it with beautiful majolica figures, which he asked Richard Luksch to decorate with symbolic farming, trade and commercial motifs. Luksch, a Secessionist, also worked on Josef Hoffmann's sanatorium (Page 116) and on two of Otto Wagner's main later projects: He created the bust of Kaiser Francis Joseph I in the Postsparkasse vestibule(Page 111) and the figures of St. Leopold and St. Severin for the Kirche Am Steinhof (Page 118).

The large globes held by atlas figures close to the roof area were removed later. Other noteworthy features are the spatial conception of the staircases and the impressively decorated ceremonial hall.

Julius and Wunibald Deininger also cooperated on the construction of the more restrained State Technical School (Federal Chemical Industry School and Testing Lab) located at Rosensteingasse 79 in the 17th district.

HAUS MOLL II
Josef Hoffmann

Wollergasse 10

Sightseeing:
None

Transportation:
Streetcar line: 37
(Geweygasse).

In May 1906, the painter Carl Moll, who was also a member of the Vienna Secession (Page 78), as was Josef Hoffmann, bought a plot of land on the Hohe Warte that was close to Hoffmann's two villas in the area, the Henneberg und Ast mansions. A comparison of the second Moll building with the first one, built only a few years before clearly shows the architect's considerable development. Its composition is more subdued than the two older buildings. Hoffmann was able to build an additional house for "his" colony on Hohe Warte over the next few years.

He drafted a first Haus Moll II project that featured irregular stone walls and a semi-circular roof, but this proposal was not approved by the

HAUS MOLL II
Josef Hoffmann

contractor. The second and finally approved project, was characterized by considerable layout
changes. He added a tower-like annex to the almost square floorplan of the main structure that
housed the kitchen on the ground floor and the
artist's studio on the upper level. Its plaster façade
separates it from the eternit-paneled main building. The wreath-shaped cornice and window
frames are accentuated with striking black and
white ornaments along the edges. Hoffmann preferred black and white in this phase of his career
since – as his biographer L. W. Rochowanski sur-
mised – there were no precursors of this style he
could cite and it reminded him of the Collalto
family seal. This family had owned a castle in
Pirnitz, Hoffmann's birthplace. The interiors were
made by the Wiener Werkstätte, where Josef
Hoffmann had acted as artistic director.

The villa was changed with additional structures in
1928 and renovated by Erich Boltenstern in
1971/72.

VILLA GESSNER
Hubert Gessner

XVIII.
Sternwarte-
straße 70

Sightseeing:
None

Transportation:
Streetcar lines: 40,
41 (Gersthof)

In 1907, Otto Wagner's pupil Hubert Gessner married his Norwegian bride, Margit Schjelderup. Their plan to start a family was probably the reason for which he decided to give up his atelier at Floragasse 6 in the 5th district and build his own home. Gessner had earned the necessary funds mainly from his work on a large construction contract to build the psychiatric clinic in Kremsier. Gessner acquired a plot of land on a then undeveloped hill close to Türkenschanzpark and built his "palazzo" with a studio on the ground floor, living area on the upper level and a laundry room, drying area and storage rooms in the attic.

The street-side of the basically ashlar-shaped structure appears to be relatively tall and narrow,

VILLA GESSNER

Hubert Gessner

although the flat projecting roof compensates for this impression. The block-like building and the cantilevered, coffer-shaped eaves are typical Wagner School motifs. The house's depth, which is underlined by the two round structures projecting into the garden (one of which was only built in 1927 on the occasion of Gessner's daughter's marriage), gave the building a surprising amount of large rooms.

The stringently symmetrical layout of the street façade is a compilation of details taken from various architectural currents: the richly trimmed roof cornice features references to antique styles, while the bay windows are an Anglo-Saxon architectural feature. The two mosaic stone vases flanking the façade, the extremely cantilevered roof and the cubic structure of the building give a Classicist air.

SANATORIUM LUITHLEN

(A student dormitory today)

Robert Örley

VIII.
Auerspergstraße 9

Sightseeing:
None

Transportation:
Subway: U2
(Rathaus)

The former Luithlen Hospital has undergone major changes on the outside and inside since it was built in 1907/08. It is one of the main examples of Robert Örley's work, a carpenter who was responsible for the construction of a large number of impressive buildings in Vienna. Josef Frank considered the hospital to be so important that he included it in his essay "Wiens moderne Architektur bis 1914" (Vienna's modern architecture until 1914) (Der Aufbau, 1926), in which he discussed 16 buildings. Franz Ottmann wrote the following about the hospital: *"The Auersperg Hospital leads towards the in fact modern purpose built complex with its three stark, sober levels that seem to be separated by broad belts. All associations with tradition have been abandoned with this design."*

The foundations for the skin and urological ailments building were laid on September 2nd, 1907.

SANATORIUM LUITHLEN

(A student dormitory today)

Robert Örley

Örley placed the rooms for seriously ill patients opposite the courtyard with baths and toilets in the immediate vicinity. The patients' rooms were originally supposed to be finished with grooved glass panels to insure privacy, but the middle section of each window was fitted with normal glass panes. Only the outer window sections were fitted with blown embossed panes, which merely created a visual effect that is continued with the geometrical pattern of the stone plinth.

The roof originally featured two ferroconcrete cupola structures at 45-degree angles in order to insure enough light reached the operation room right behind them despite the building's alignment facing north. The facility was inaugurated on July 20th, 1908.

The cupolas and glass canopy were removed in 1964, when the building was re-fitted as a students' hostel.

KÄRNTNER-BAR (LOOS-BAR)
Adolf Loos

I.
Kärntner
Durchgang

Sightseeing:
During opening
hours

Transportation:
Subways: U1, U3
(Stephansplatz)

Adolf Loos, who had lived in the United States in his youth, brought his experiences there to bear on the construction of the Kärntner-Bar. It was the second locale after Café Museum (1899) that he designed the interiors for. He was also responsible for building the Café Capua on Johannesgasse in 1913, but this coffeehouse no longer exists.

The narrow portal of the Kärntner-Bar achieves its effect via the unorthodox combination of a poster-like writing space and colorful glass applications in the shape of the American flag as well as fine Skyros marble. Loos only had three blocks of stone at his disposition for the four marble columns. He

KÄRNTNER-BAR (LOOS-BAR)
Adolf Loos

had one block cut diagonally and set the halves at the outer ends of the portal.

On the inside, the visitor is fascinated by an economy of space that is taken to its limits in the small, 4,45 x 6,15 meter locale, without neglecting the elegance a bar requires. By using mirrored zones on the upper paneling, Loos achieved an impressive visual expansion of the small bar room, without imposing on the guests with reflections. Valuable materials such as onyx, marble, brass and mahogany set the tone. Even the beam in front of the bar (from barre, thus a "bar") is made of mahogany. The transom facing the street consists of a grid with square, thinly cut onyx panels. The coffered ceiling is made of yellow-white marble pieces. The once colorful, flower-patterned seat covers were replaced with red leatherette.

After years of neglect, the Kärntner-Bar was renovated and restored by Hermann Czech and Burkhardt Rukschcio between 1985 and 1989.

LUEGER-GEDÄCHTNISKIRCHE
(ZENTRALFRIEDHOFSKIRCHE)

Max Hegele

Sightseeing:
Open
to the public

Transportation:
Streetcar lines:
71, 72
(Zentralfriedhof,
2nd gate)

Max Hegele studied under Carl von Hasenauer at
the Academy of Fine Arts (Page 42) and taught at
the State Trade School in Vienna. In 1900, he won
the competition to build supplementary buildings
at the Viennese Zentralfriedhof (Main Cemetery)
in 1874. Over the following years, he built the
2nd gate, the second funeral parlor and the Zentralfriedhof church – as the focal point of the entire
cemetery.

Although Hegele cited historical examples, despite
the unusual location of the towers at the back, the
church is a significant example of Jugendstil architecture.

The oft-heard assumption that Hegele copied
Otto Wagner's church at Steinhof (Page 118) is not
accurate. Hegele's planning went back to 1899 and
the Steinhof church competition was only held in
1902. The Zentralfriedhof church is designed to

LUEGER-GEDÄCHTNISKIRCHE
(ZENTRALFRIEDHOFSKIRCHE)
Max Hegele

accommodate twice as many visitors as Wagner's institution church. The ribbed cupola of Hegele's church and the substructure form an integral unit, giving the entire building cohesive, three-dimensional outline. On the inside, Hegele took the effect of the 39-meter-high cupola (58.5 meters high outside) into consideration, unlike Otto Wagner.

A number of respected artists worked on the interiors of the church, these are some of them: Carl Wollek, Theodor Charlemont, Josef Heu, Josef Breitner, Arthur Kaan. There were also a few who had worked for Otto Wagner, such as Othmar Schimkowitz and Leopold Forstner.

The tomb of Viennese Mayor Karl Lueger is located in the crypt of the church dedicated to St. Karl Borromäus.

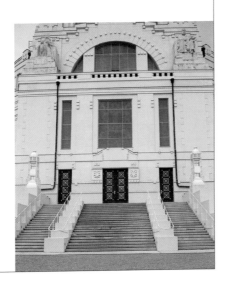

SKIN TUBERCULOSIS HOSPITAL
Otto Wagner

The skin tuberculosis hospital in the 16th district is one of Otto Wagner's last realized buildings. *"With the hospital, a giant complex, he is realizing his vision of the ideal hygienic-sanitary facility. Most of all, it promises to become a building of great simplicity and harmony."* (Joseph August Lux) Wagner created H-shaped ground plans for the skin tuberculosis facility. He located the façade on the connecting wing, giving the hospital a symmetric ceremonial forecourt. The layout of the main façade shows the conflict between Wagner "the functionalist" and Wagner "the classicist."(Friedrich Achleitner) The architect made use of traditional styles (rustic elements, structured stone, pilaster sequence), which he reduced to their basic forms or only suggested, creating an almost abstract effect. One of the façade's main elements are bordering ornaments made of small blue glass panes. He used them to, *"give the buildings a long life cycle free of repairs and to give them a cheerful, proper appearance."* (Otto Wagner, Explanatory Report)

Wagner also explored new possibilities with the distribution of patient wards. *"The patient rooms*

XVI.
Montléarstraße 37,
Wilhelminenspital,
Pavillon 24

Sightseeing:
None

Transportation:
Streetcar line: 46
(Rankgasse)

SKIN TUBERCULOSIS HOSPITAL

Otto Wagner

facing south include the following innovation: next to the distribution of patients according to sex and age, the number of patients per room will be kept as low as possible, taking into account the patient's sense of individuality. Deep rooms with beds on both sides were avoided for economic reasons, but also to keep patients from having to look into the light." (Otto Wagner, Explanatory Report)

HAUS AST
Josef Hoffmann

XIX.
Steinfeldgasse 2
Wollergasse 12

Sightseeing:
None

Transportation:
Streetcar line: 37
(Hohe Warte)

The villa for the building contractor Eduard Ast was Josef Hoffman's last contribution to the "Villenkolonie Hohe Warte." Hoffmann used the corner location between his two earlier Spitzer houses (Page 98) and Moll II (Page 128) by connecting an elevated terrace to the base course of the building. He built the villa on an almost square layout, the stereometrics of which are only interrupted by the semi-circular, curved staircase. *"Hoffmann's glib rhetoric in terms of classical architectural vocabulary is once again visible here in a relatively unorthodox manner, such as the grooves on the exterior of the entire villa."* (August Sarnitz) The grooves and many other shaped decoration elements were supposed to demonstrate cement's versatility as a construction material, a view propagated by the villa contractor in his construction projects. *"I envy the structural engineer who has the good fortune of being allowed to make one of Hoffmann's buildings a reality under the guidance of the great artist himself. He is allowed to watch in admi-*

HAUS AST

Josef Hoffmann

*ration as Hoffmann masters modern construction mate-
rials and grasps all their possibilities almost intuitively.
And he sees how Hoffmann creates new forms of
beauty with these new options that are the product of
his decency and magnanimity."* (Eduard Ast)

Hoffmann counterbalanced the grooves derived
from classical column structures with a heavy, very
profiled wreath-shaped cornice. He decorated the
windows of the uppermost level with sculpted
festoons.

The villa was the home of Alma Mahler-Werfel
and her third husband the writer Franz Werfel.

MIETHÄUSER DÖBLERGASSE
– NEUSTIFTGASSE

Otto Wagner

VII.

Neustiftgasse 40/
Döblergasse 2,
Döblergasse 4

Sightseeing:
Döblergasse 4
by appointment

Transportation:
Streetcar line: 46
Bus: 13A
(Strozzigasse)

The two metropolitan apartment buildings located on neighboring plots on the narrow alley of Döblergasse are the last two Otto Wagner projects that were built. Wagner once again acted as his own contractor here, which, as usual, gave him the unrestricted ability to realize his vision. His last city apartment was at Döblergasse 4, and he also passed away here in 1918, a fact that is commemorated with a plaque next to the entrance designed by his pupil Carl Reinhart. The apartment has been the home of the Academy of Fine Art's (Page 42) Otto Wagner archive since 1985, and the remnants of the original wall décor can still be admired here today.

MIETHÄUSER DÖBLERGASSE
– NEUSTIFTGASSE

Otto Wagner

Otto Wagner's concept of modern apartment buildings as a "Zellenkonglomerat" (conglomerate of cells) was expressed much more clearly with the exterior of this building than with his Wienzeile apartment buildings (Page 80). He had abandoned the palace scheme with its piano nobile emphasis that was still common among other such structures at the time long ago. For Wagner, the uniformity among apartment buildings resulted from the ever-growing similarities in people's lifestyles.

In constructing the building at Neustiftgasse 40, Wagner strove to create panel-like façade surfaces by covering the surfaces of the main floors with plaster grooves before separating them on the edge of buildings with fugues. He took his guiding functionalist principle that every ornament has to be justified with a purpose to new extremes here: the building address, "Neustiftgasse 40", is written with little black glass tiles that are embedded in the plaster wall.

For Wagner's biographer Joseph August Lux, the youthfully fresh buildings the septuagenarian architect created on Döblergasse once again proved that he was immune to passing of time.

DRUCK- UND VERLAGSANSTALT "VORWÄRTS"

Hubert and Franz Gessner

V.
Rechte
Wienzeile 97

Sightseeing:
During opening
hours

Transportation:
Subway: U4,
Bus: 13A
(Kettenbrücken-
gasse)

The Social Democratic Party's continuous growth
made it necessary to keep finding larger quarters
for the political movement's administration. For
this reason, in 1909, the party acquired the three-
story house at Rechte Wienzeile 57 that had been
built in 1877 by the civil engineer Weigang for
the owner of the plot, Schönbichler. The party
then hired Hubert Gessner to refurbish the entire building and make space in the courtyard for a
printing shop. The façade Gessner designed for
the side of the building facing Rechte Wienzeile

DRUCK- UND VERLAGSANSTALT "VORWÄRTS"

Hubert and Franz Gessner

was the first to display the pathetic architectural language that was characteristic of Social Democratic architecture between the two world wars. Overall, the shapes Gessner chose for the façade are examples of his effort to create architecture that stood apart from the bourgeois buildings of the period, such as worker's home building in Vienna's tenth district. The façade and its silhouette on the Rechte Wienzeile were considered a symbol of the Social Democratic Worker's Party even after WWII.

Anton Hanak's colossal fascia figures that symbolize a male and female worker, *"elevate the building to a new level, both idealistically and factually in reference to the surrounding buildings since it is the birthplace of the Socialist Workers' Movement. In addition to this, the tension created by the combination of functional, sober structuring, the building's expressive-ideological statement of purpose and its Neo-Classicist elements make it an important precursor of the Viennese public housing projects of the period between the World Wars."* (Eckart Vancsa)

LOOSHAUS

(formerly Geschäftshaus Goldman & Salatsch)

Adolf Loos

I.
Michaelerplatz 3

Sightseeing:
Only on the
ground floor
during opening
hours

Transportation:
Subways: U1, U3
(Stephansplatz,
Herrengasse)

Adolf Loos included elements from the surrounding older buildings on the sparingly decorated façade of the Goldman & Salatsch commercial building. The only precious ornament was the richly veined, green Cipollino marble used on the portal. The placement of the four green Cipollino columns was Loos' reaction to the Michaelerkirche portico across the way. The generously proportioned exedra of the Hofburg's Michaelertrakt (Page

LOOSHAUS

(formerly Geschäftshaus Goldman & Salatsch)

Adolf Loos

66) across the way is reflected in the diagonally recessed entrance. The height of the marble-paneled portal area and the green-finished copper plating of the roof are references to the Hofburg as well. The sophisticated profile of the projecting eaves ledge cites the Biedermeier Michaelerhaus apartment building on the opposite side of Kohlmarkt.

The plain upper level façade design caused one of the greatest architecture scandals in international architecture history, which made a lasting impression on the interested public that is still felt today. Finally, as a compromise, flower boxes were added to some of the "house without eyebrow's" windows.

The actual heart of the building is the interior of the commercial space. The complicated distribution of space made ferroconcrete-building technology necessary in order to realize Loos' vision. The young Viennese civil engineer Ernst Epstein assisted him. The walls of the compartmentalized rooms featured valuable mahogany and mirrored paneling and the wall lamps and staircase railings are made of brass. The marble-paneled stairway and white tile finish of the courtyard are also noteworthy.

The architect Burkhart Rukschcio completed an exemplary renovation of the building only a few years ago.

HEILIG-GEIST-KIRCHE (PFARRKIRCHE SCHMELZ)

Josef Plečnik

XVI.
Herbststraße 82

Sightseeing:
Open
to the public

Transportation:
Streetcar line: 9,
Subway: U6
(Koppstraße)

Josef Plečnik's last Viennese project pioneered new urban construction, programmatic, technical construction and space conception solutions. The unusual assignment of building a "Missionsstätte christlich-sozialer Bestrebungen" (mission for Christian-Social endeavors) with an assembly hall, parish and apartment building in the middle of a workers' district was unprecedented at the time. The "Verein zur Erbauung und Ausstattung einer katholischen Kirche" (Association for the Construction and Furnishing of a Catholic Church) acted as the contractor. Plečnik had many tortuous discussions, after which the architect was forced to make a series of layout changes. Due to financial difficulties, the project program and the building were never completed.

Plečnik made use of the new construction and

HEILIG-GEIST-KIRCHE (PFARRKIRCHE SCHMELZ)

Josef Plečnik

1910

aesthetic possibilities ferroconcrete offered to develop a new form of the basilica, by replacing the arcades of the lateral naves with two over 20-meter-long freely suspended "bridge struts." The skylight above was also widened, allowing for improved visibility and acoustics.

The new material allowed the architect to use a tight column arrangement in the crypt that brought back memories of the dark rooms in Roman lower churches using contemporary architectural methods. The thin pillars and their thin capitals are the result of ferroconcrete's properties. Their shape is a reference to Czech cubist forms. Plečnik created an atmosphere of warmth and security with the material texture contrasts (fine graining, blasted smooth surfaces, added reddish brick gravel). Franz Ferdinand, the heir to the throne, who also condemned Otto Wagner's church Am Steinhof (Page 118) deemed the building *"a hodgepodge of a Russian bath + horse stable + Venus Temple."*

HAUS STEINER
Adolf Loos

This building is one of Adolf Loos' most famous projects along with the Haus am Michaelerplatz (Page 146), and is also considered a key example of modern architecture. The house's cube-like appearance with its smooth, white walls and the strict proportions of the window openings foreshadow what later became the "International Style," although the architect energetically rejected this view.

In building Haus Steiner, Loos faced the same problems with the construction authorities that arose with respect to the "Goldman & Salatsch" building on Michaelerplatz. The eaves of the house had to be at a certain height, yet Loos managed to turn this constriction into a surprising building element, without sacrificing space. He created a three-story house whose upper levels were balanced by a semi-circular structure in front of the entrance. On the garden side, the façade seems to be that of a four-story house with the cellar. The windows are of different shapes and the pediment-like two outer window axes underline the strict symmetry of the structure. On the inside, the house

XIII.
St. Veit-Gasse 10

Sightseeing:
None

Transportation:
Streetcar line: 58
(Hummelgasse)

HAUS STEINER

Adolf Loos

shows early features of the one-family house ground plan Loos developed a few years later, despite the overlapping levels he was forced to use here due to the varying height of the individual stories.

The semicircular structure was removed in the fifties, but the house was completely restored with all its original features by Burkhart Rukschcio in 1994.

Lilly Steiner, the painter who commissioned the building, located her studio behind the large street-side window. Her daughter Eva was the wife of Albertina Director Otto Benesch.

STRUDELHOFSTIEGE

Theodor Jäger

IX.
Strudelhofstiege

Sightseeing:
Open
to the public

Transportation:
Streetcar lines: 37,
38, 40, 41, 42,
(Sensengasse)

The 9th district's geomorphologic structure is uneven. Liechtensteinstraße, which used to be a Danube tributary, lies next to a slope. It separates what used to be meadows and alluvial land from the terrace-like incline of this part of the ninth district. This fault had to be compensated with steep streets (e. g. Berggasse), ramps and flights of staps. The Strudelhofstiege is indisputably the most imposing and artistically valuable example of such a solution. It was named after the "Strudelhof" building (built in 1690, originally at Strudelhof-gasse 1–5, 2–10) that in turn took its name from the Imperial Court painter Peter Strudel.

Theodor Jäger, an architect who worked for the Viennese construction authorities between 1900 and 1930, designed the Strudelhofstiege. Baroque double staircases inspired his design. He created a combination of ramps, steps and terraces that invite the visitor to stay for a while and enjoy the view. Due to the difference in height and the double staircase, visitors are constantly changing directions horizontally and vertically. Hence climbing the steps becomes a conscious act and spatial movement.

The fountain emanating from a two-part basin on the wall is the centerpiece of the design. The upper basin on the stair wall features a water spouting head mask. On the first staircase level, the water streams out of a fish mouth into a mosaic paneled niche.

However, it was not its clever architectural solution to the given topography or its design that gave it its fame, but the novel by Heimito von Doderer, who lived close by on Währinger Straße.

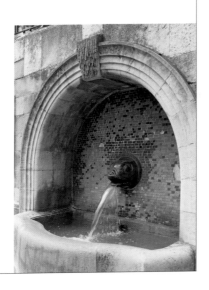

HAUS IN DER COBENZLGASSE (HAUS HOCH)

Oskar Strnad, Oskar Wlach

XIX.
Cobenzlgasse 71

Sightseeing:
None

Transportation:
Bus: 38A
(Grinzinger
Feuerwache)

Oskar Strnad was born in Vienna in 1879. He studied under Carl König at the Technical University in Vienna, from which he received his doctorate in 1904 for his work on "Early Christian Art." He became a professor at the Vienna Art Trade School, today's University of Applied Arts (Page 40), in 1909.

Strnad mainly worked as an interior designer. His designs (theater buildings) and War Ministry, his Crematory (Page 182) competition entry in Vienna and the proposed League of Nations palace in Geneva were never built. He also participated in community project construction a number of times in Socialist Vienna, such as the "Winarsky-Hof" (Page 200), and collaborated with Max Reinhardt on a number of productions as a set designer.

The house for Oskar Hoch on Cobenzlgasse in

HAUS IN DER COBENZLGASSE (HAUS HOCH)
Oskar Strnad, Oskar Wlach

Grinzing was the result of a joint effort with his partner, Oskar Wlach, but without the usual participation of Josef Frank. However, the building is nonetheless the first of the group's projects that veers away from Secessionism (Page 78). Instead, it re-introduces pre-March Classicism and Biedermeier themes. The unusual garden-side orientation of the columned portico underlines the reflection of Classicist styles.

The plot's location on a slope made the use of a multi-segment staircase necessary. This gives the third and last floor of the house and the terrace the appearance of a level structure from the garden perspective.

At the time, the house, which appears timeless today, was considered a radical/revolutionary building. So much so that the responsible authorities were initially unwilling to grant a construction permit since the house represented a *"coarse disfigurement of the townscape."*

VILLA WAGNER II
Otto Wagner

XIV.
Hüttelberg-
straße 28

Sightseeing:
None

Transportation:
Streetcar line: 49
(Hütteldorf),
Bus: 148
(Campingplatz
Wien West 1)

Otto Wagner drafted preliminary plans for a villa for educational purposes here as early as 1905. However, he ultimately had the building constructed with minor changes as a retreat for his wife once she became a widow (she was 18 years younger than her husband) in 1912/13. However, she died in the villa in 1915, three years before Wagner died. Wagner sold the house in 1916.

The fact that the house is in the immediate vicinity of the first villa he built in 1886 (Page 62) encourages a direct comparison. A quarter of a century of experience lies between the two houses. His development from a Neo-Renaissance to a modern style, from a historical to his own personal form of décor (Ottokar Uhl), is recognizable. This evolution would not have been possible without improved building technology.

VILLA WAGNER II
Otto Wagner

Ferroconcrete construction was used on the cubic structure's narrow, high, rectangular, flush openings. Like, *"a brim without a hat,"* (Friedrich Achleitner) was the description of the wreath-shaped cornice, which is still reminiscent of Renaissance style. The décor is limited to slender, blue glass strips and aluminum nails to trim the edges and accentuate the main floor similar to those used on the buildings built at the same time on Döblergasse (Page 142). The window over the lateral projecting entrance with a Perseus and Medusa head motif were designed by Kolo Moser and made by Leopold Forstner's Wiener Mosaik-werkstätte. This company had created Wagner's high altar mosaic for the Kirche Am Steinhof (Page 118) earlier.

The dispute as to whether this house is symmetrical or not becomes irrelevant in view of this masterpiece of *"summarized reduction and concentration."* (Friedrich Achleitner)

HAUS HORNER
Adolf Loos

XIII.
Nothartgasse 7

Sightseeing:
None

Transportation:
Subway: U4
(Unter St. Veit),
Bus: 55B
(Tolstoigasse)

At first glance, the building's unique roof shape is reminiscent of the Villa (Page 150) Steiner Adolf Loos built only a few years earlier. However, it was built under entirely different circumstances. Throughout his life, Loos worked on famous projects for both wealthy contractors, for which he created expansive structures using expensive materials, as well as low-cost housing. An example of this is the Siedlung am Heuberg project and the twin buildings of the Wiener Werkbundsiedlung. The single-family house he built for Helene Horner on a surface area of only 10 x 11 is one the buildings he completed with the most inexpensive materials. In order to save space on the inside, the house only has load-bearing exterior walls. Loos was following his principle that a wall should only serve as a support for the interior or for protection. The continuous, three-meter-high residential floors are only divided by plaster wall separators between the respective rooms. Loos

HAUS HORNER

Adolf Loos

1912

made use of the plot's location on a slope to build a servant's apartment next to the heating, garage and laundry room in the basement.

To make better use of the uppermost floor and the attic, Loos covered the house with a large barrel-shaped copper sheet roof that dominates the entire building. *"From the street, the structure seems to be a humble little house with a structured roof. From the garden, it seems to be a mansion-like cube with a cleverly mounted, almost dematerialized barrel roof."* (Friedrich Achleitner)

VILLA WUSTL
Robert Örley

Sightseeing:
None

Transportation:
Streetcar line: 58
(Wenzgasse)

The palace of the Duke of Braunschweig had to be torn down in 1912 in order to make space on a plot that was shaped like a slightly imperfect rectangle for the construction of the screw manufacturer Richard Wustl's new villa. The site is located between Auhofstraße und Hietzinger Hauptstraße in the 13th district. Only parts of the palace's glass house survived and were incorporated in the new building by the architect. Although the villa's exterior remained unchanged, the interior was later subjected to major changes, the most painful of which was the loss of the central hall with its gallery.

The modern appearance of the cubic villa is crowned by a high two-level pyramid-shaped roof. This makes the basic conception of the house as the combination of a cube with a pyramid clear. The skylight along the entire roof helps dematerialize this area.

The music room, a traditional element of Viennese

VILLA WUSTL
Robert Örley

19th century architecture that was masterfully executed a number of times, is a jewel. The wooden paneling, the umbrella-like folds of the stucco ceiling and the central chandelier blend together creating an inseparable unit.

Every connoisseur of 19th and early 20th century will be surprised to see the two mosaic vases on the driveway up from Hietzinger Hauptstraße. They are analogous to the vases in front of the Secession (Page 79) including the bronze turtles *"The architectural and spatial conception is a remarkable feat of integration between Palladian stringency and a British sense of freedom in the relation between spaces, including the outside."* (Friedrich Achleitner)

BUCHHANDLUNG MANZ
Adolf Loos

I.
Kohlmarkt 16

Sightseeing:
During opening hours

Transportation:
Subway: U3
(Herrengasse)

A few months after Adolf Loos had finished his main Viennese project, the "Goldman & Salatsch" building on Michaelerplatz (Page 146), he built the locale for Universitätsbuchhandlung Manz (Manz University Booksellers). The store's owner, Dr. Robert Stein, had Loos design the interiors of his apartment on Pfarrhofgasse in 1913.

Loos designed the portal, which can still be admired today, and two offices on the first floor. Despite the narrow 6-meter portal, Loos managed to create 11-meter-long store windows by building a long passageway leading to the entrance. The impression of extensive surface was achieved with the symmetric portal design, its wide passageway in the middle and the flanking showcases. The white veins of the black marble, which once again shows that Loos was the son of a sculptor, contrast with the brass lettering on the translucent glass panels, giving it the appearance of a horizontal strut. Loos used mahogany paneling on the back walls of the lateral store windows. The lavishly decorated, gold-plated company name lettering on black marble create a particularly pretentious and contrasting effect. Bronze flower boxes top off the portal.

The passageway's lit, coffered translucent glass ceiling with its slender square mullions, gives the potential customer the feeling he is already inside while still outside, inviting him or her to stay a bit and enter the store.

Loos modified the furniture he had designed for the apartment of Eugen Stössler in 1899 for the bookstore's offices. To provide storage space, Loos created tables consisting of a round wood slab resting on three grooved columns set on triangular marble base plates.

HAUS SCHEU
Adolf Loos

The two lower levels of the innovative three-front building that was considered provocative at the time, housed the generously sized apartment of the lawyer and Social Democratic municipal politician Dr. Gustav Scheu (1875–1935), who was the city councillor in charge of residential construction from 1919 until 1920. His wife, Helene Scheu-Riess (1880–1970), was a writer and publisher and participated actively in the Austrian women's movement until 1934. A separate apartment on the 2nd floor can be reached via a separate street entrance followed by a narrow spiral staircase.

The residential building with the step-like, terraced façade was built on a surface area of 11 x 16 meters. The two bedrooms on the east side are recessed by 4 meters in correspondence to the forcefully structured block. By using flat roofs, Loos created terraces, gaining open spaces that compensated for the surface covered by the house's structure. Loos developed the varying window sizes in combination with a system of corresponding modules.

The house's interior doesn't reveal its layout immediately, although the smooth transition between the residential areas is remarkable. These rooms and the chimney corner, a familiar Anglo-Saxon element that Loos enjoyed using, are all on one level.

In order to be granted a permit by the construction authorities, Loos had to guarantee the house would be covered by vegetation at a later stage and make a proposal for a building on the neighboring plot. However, the project was never built. The building was completely refurbished and restored to its original state by Heinz Neumann and Sepp Frank in 1978/79. The overgrowth today gives the structure its actually intended appearance.

XIII.
Larochegasse 3

Sightseeing:
one

Transportation:
Streetcar lines: 58, 60 (Fleschgasse, Wenzgasse)

HAUS SCHEU

Adolf Loos

1912

HÄUSER IN DER WILBRANDTGASSE
Josef Frank, Oskar Wlach, Oskar Strnad

XIX.
Wilbrandtgasse 3
und 11

Sightseeing:
None

Transportation:
Streetcar line: 41,
(Scheibenberg-
straße)

Josef Frank was born in Baden, right outside
Vienna in 1885. He trained at the Technical
University in Vienna, where he studied under the
conservative Carl König and received his doctorate for his dissertation, "The Original Design of
the Religious Buildings of Leone Battista Alberti."
The contract to design the interior for the
Museum of East Asian Art in Cologne in 1912 had
a major influence on his further activities as an
architect.

As the coordinating architect, Frank planned an
ensemble of a number of town houses on
Wilbrandtgasse in 1913 in cooperation with his
two contemporaries, Oskar Wlach and Oskar

HÄUSER IN DER WILBRANDTGASSE
Josef Frank, Oskar Wlach, Oskar Strnad

Strnad. Only two were ultimately built. The house at No. 3 is the better preserved of the two and also the more noteworthy. The project contractors were Dr. Emil and Agnes Scholl. The building reflects the architect's ideas on architectural design, which he only articulated in writing years later. The basically symmetric façade only reveals its minor asymmetric aspects on second glance. These are intended to give the house an air of coincidence, as if it had grown there. The cubic building is almost completely devoid of ornamentation, which gives the visitor an indication of the solutions that came with the International Style later. However, the traces of custom construction elements weren't symmetrized, they were still consciously displayed. (Andreas Lehne) The street-side, nearly square facade reminds the visitor of Haus Moller (Page 214), built by Adolf Loos ten years later.

The house built for Oskar und Hanny Straus at No. 11 was subjected to major changes (a hipped roof, window openings, balcony enlargement).

VILLA SKYWA-PRIMAVESI
Josef Hoffmann

1913

XIII.
Gloriette-
gasse 14–16

Sightseeing:
None

Transportation:
Streetcar line: 60
(Gloriettegasse),
Subway: U4
(Hietzing),

Josef Hoffmann's extremely generously dimensioned estate and villa is considered the zenith and culminating moment of refined Viennese residential life on the eave of World War I. The industrialist Robert Primavesi had the villa built for his "partner in his later years," Josefine Skywa.

The building is one of the most important examples of Hoffman's work along with the Purkersdorf sanatorium (Page 116) and Palais Stoclet in Brussels. The extent to which the former friends Adolf Loos and Josef Hoffmann, as *"representatives of a critical bourgeoisie and one devoted to the pleasures of life"* (Friedrich Achleitner), had become estranged becomes clear when one compares this

VILLA SKYWA-PRIMAVESI
Josef Hoffmann

villa to the Loos villas built only a few years before in the same district, Haus Steiner (Page 150)
and Haus Scheu (Page 164). The close wall surfaces dissolve into shimmering, multi-fold layers
in Hoffmann's building and Hoffmann preferred
to build by merging differing structures. Loos, on
the other hand, used one dominating shape.
Hoffmann concentrated on underlining the building's purpose with its exterior design, whereas
Loos concentrated on the interiors.

The street-side façade is symmetrically designed
and features sculpted pillar ornaments and gable
decorations created by Anton Hanak. The garden
façade features differ significantly. Recesses and
projecting elements as well as varying terrace levels
are the dominating characteristics. The most important structural features are the grooved wall
pillars and the wreath-shaped cornice with its
delicate relief decorations. The park-like garden
contains a number of architecturally remarkable
annexes (a glasshouse, a garage and gate keeper's
quarters as well as a "Little Tea Temple").

VILLA LEMBERGER

Jan Kotěra

XIX.

Grinzinger
Allee 50–52

Sightseeing:
None

Transportation:
Streetcar line: 38,
(An den langen
Lüssen)

Jan Kotěra was a pupil and associate of Otto Wagner between 1894 and 1897. After a trip to Rome, he was selected to succeed Friedrich Ohmann at the Art and Crafts Trade School in Prague, where he remained until he was appointed to teach at the Academy in Prague. He was a professor of architectural composition there until his death in 1923. Kotěra is generally considered the father of modern Czech architecture. The most important architects of the twenties and thirties such as Josef Gočar, Otakar Novotný und Bohuslav Fuchs, were his pupils. His mission of adapting historical elements for use in modern architecture is clearly visible in many of the details of his only Viennese project. Kotěra built Villa

VILLA LEMBERGER

Jan Kotěra

Lemberger during the final stage of his career when he began to prefer classical forms, as did many other Wagner pupils.

In 1914, well before he left Vienna, he designed a villa complex for two families on Grinzingerallee in Grinzing, Vienna's 19th district. The imposing facility consists of two independent buildings and features a ceremonial forecourt space that opens onto the street. A one-story pergola flanks the residential building on the right The main unit was built surrounding a small courtyard. The expressionist asymmetry of the pilaster structure on the ground level contrasts with the ornamental, ochre brick paneling used on the upper level. This feature helps give it an attic-like appearance. Plaster and layered brickwork add liveliness to the façades.

WOHN- UND GESCHÄFTSHAUS "FÜRSTENHOF"

Rudolf Perco

II.
Praterstraße 25

Sightseeing:
None

Transportation:
Subway: U 1
(Nestroyplatz)

Rudolf Perco was born in Görz (Gorizia, Friuli/ Italy) in 1884. He came to Vienna and studied under Otto Wagner from 1906 until 1910. At the same time, he also worked at Hubert Gessner's studio. He worked on Viennese community housing projects a number of times between the two wars, and the most important example of his oeuvre is the Engelsplatz-Hof (Page 226), which he built between 1929/33.

Perco completed construction on the residential and commercial facility on Praterstraße 25 – the entire complex comprises buildings on Praterstraße 25, 25a and Zirkusgasse 8 – shortly before WWI broke out. It was the first project Perco actually completed according to his own plans. The impressive, Neo-Classicist building was named "Fürstenhof" (Earl's Court).

The building now lacks the original high roof, which influences the overall effect of the entire complex. The almost cubic-shaped ledge achieves a striking effect over the façade, which is dominated by the central double-oriel loggia layout. The smooth façade facing Zirkusgasse with the projecting cornice resembles those on Otto Wagner's late buildings.

The Italian sculptor Alfonso Canciani, who had already created the sculpted ornaments for Max Fabiani's Haus Artaria am Kohlmarkt (Page 88), was hired to create the reliefs for the attic level (allegory of the four seasons). This shows the loyalty among Italian artists in Vienna before WWI began. Perco built another residential and commercial building on the corner of Taborstraße and Obere Donaustraße, close to Fürstenhof, in this period. Carl Appel renovated the building, which had been damaged during the war, and made a series of changes. It was replaced by a Hans Hollein-designed high rise in 1999/2000.

ZENTRALSPARKASSE MARIAHILF-NEUBAU
(formerly Anglo-Österreichische Bank)

Adolf Loos

Adolf Loos responded to Otto Wagner's Postsparkasse (Page 110), which was considered a progressive building, by stressing conservative, bourgeois values such as earnestness, discretion and longevity in his work. Loos brought all his knowledge of psychologically-based structural solutions to bear in designing this business portal, as he had done for earlier commercial projects (e.g. Knize (Page 122) und Manz (Page 162)). These heightened the importance and presence of the entrance and achieved a suggestive effect.

He applied black granite paneling to the narrow, only five-meter-wide and eleven-meter high portal that spans both the ground and mezzanine levels. The grooved Lisene edging flanking the entrance and the broad block lettering create the impression of a horizontal beam, giving the portal its Neo-Classical character. The customer enters the dark foyer, and continues through rooms of differing size before reaching the high-ceilinged, brightly illuminated teller area that only receives light from the milk-glass-paneled roof. 'This "Temple Hall" elevated money matters to a cult.' (Friedrich Achleitner) Loos nonetheless managed to create a comfortable atmosphere with the dark leather cushions of the oak benches and by providing writing surfaces within the marble-paneled wall structure of the hall. White marble panels, gray pilasters and mirrored effects in the upper niches of the paneling emphasize the walls' structure.

In 1927, the Zentralsparkasse der Gemeinde Wien (Central Savings Bank of the City of Vienna) bought the facility from its original owners. The bank was only recognized as Loos' project at the end of the sixties, and completely refurbished and restored in 1973.

VII.
Mariahilfer
Straße 70

Sightseeing:
During open
hours

Transportation:
Subway: U3
(Neubau)

ZENTRALSPARKASSE MARIAHILF-NEUBAU

(formerly Anglo-Österreichische Bank)

Adolf Loos

1914

WOHNHAUS WATTMANNGASSE
"SCHOKOLADEHAUS"

Ernst Lichtblau

XIII.
Wattmanngasse 29

Sightseeing:
None

Transportation:
Subway: U4,
Buses: 56B, 58B
(Tiroler Gasse)

Ernst Lichtblau was born in Vienna in 1883. He trained under Otto Wagner at the Academy of Fine Arts (Page 42), at which time he was the only Jewish student. In 1905, after his studies, he spent time traveling to Italy, Germany and Bosnia. He taught technical drawing for furniture carpentry at the State Trade School on Schellinggasse from 1906 until 1914.

The meerschaum pipe manufacturer Dr. Hoffman contracted Lichtblau for the project. The unusual design of the façade, which features dark brown, partly sculpted ceramic paneling that links the windows to create horizontal stripes, also features a high wreath-shaped cornice. These elements gave it its nickname, "Schokoladehaus". The vertical rectangular ceramic fields between the windows show folkloric and expressively dressed figures in a thriving, exotic plant world. These motifs could be interpreted as over-sized meerschaum pipe carvings, an indication of the owner's profession. However, it can also be seen as a reaction to Czech cubism or, due to the horizontal layering, as the vanguard of the New Objectivity that was to come in the twenties. The ceramic paneling used by Wagner pupils and associates on other projects (Portois & Fix by Max Fabiani) are derivative of Otto Wagner's Majolikahaus on Linke Wienzeile (Page 80). The sculpted ornaments Richard Luksch created for the façade of the Trade Academy designed by Wunibald Deininger (Page 162) strongly resemble those of the Schokoladehaus." The building's major architectural innovation is its horizontal emphasis.

ZEISS-WERKE
Robert Örley

XIV.
Abbegasse I

Sightseeing:
None

Transportation:
Streetcar line: 46
Bus: 48A
(Waidäckergasse)

In the middle of WWI, Robert Örley built a production site for the German precision optics manufacturer at an extremely exposed location. The visual reference to the Kirche Am Steinhof (Page 118) built ten years earlier by Otto Wagner and its strikingly profiled observatory dome give the building an almost "religious" air that corresponds to the institution church. Despite, or because of, its appearance as a production and administration facility – in accordance with the attitudes of the time – the impression is one of form defined by performance. (Friedrich Achleitner)
The massiveness of the building block is underli-

ZEISS-WERKE
Robert Örley

ned by its consistent height, the octagonal layout of its fronts and the pyramid-like structural height increments. The ferroconcrete structure stresses the building's mundane purpose, creating a contrast to the religious appearance.

The large, imposing assembly hall on the upper-most level is supported by wide ferroconcrete pillars and can only be recognized by the row of porthole-like windows on the outside. Örley used glass panels (now covered) on the slanted roofs to ensure better natural light. Shutter elements mounted lengthwise could be set in different positions to adjust the amount of light. The venti-lation was also technically noteworthy since it required a sophisticated natural airflow solution.

The precision and simplicity of some of the con-struction details are still intriguing today, such as the composite wood windows on the outside, the glass metal structures on the inside as well as the riveted banisters and fixtures.

HAUS STRASSER
Adolf Loos

XIII.
Kupelwieser-
gasse 28

Sightseeing:
None

Transportation:
Streetcar line: 58
(Fleschgasse)

Adolf Loos made changes so major to the building originally commissioned by the Österreichische Heimstätten-Gesellschaft that the original substance of the structure can barely be recognized. He removed parts of the outer walls, tore down the staircase and removed most of the inside walls as well as some ceilings of the ground floor level. He also added an attic level.

Haus Strasser gives the visitor an indication of the space and layout concepts the architect developed to full effect in the construction of Haus Rufer (Page 188), which he built four years later. The reduced, compartmentalized spaces on the inside correspond to the façade's design, which is congruous to the space constellation. This objectification eliminated varying street and garden façade features. Loos later abandoned this stringency in his façade designs and reverted to more symmetrical arrangements.

The shallow barrel-shaped copper sheet roof

HAUS STRASSER
Adolf Loos

reminds the visitor of Haus Steiner (Page 150) and Haus Horner (Page 158).

The building's accessibility and layout, which already featured a full range of progressively larger room sizes, are remarkable. Starting from a group of low, small rooms (porch, hall, closet), one continues along a path interrupted by a series of right angles into the innermost core of the house. This core consists of the dining room with its porous "filled-in green onyx" and figure-shaped frieze as well as the music podium and its visual centerpiece, a monolithic marble column with a flat stylized capital. Many other fixed paneling elements and furniture pieces made of valuable wood types have been preserved.

KREMATORIUM
Clemens Holzmeister

XI.
Simmeringer
Hauptstraße 337

Sightseeing:
Open
to the public

Transportation:
Streetcar lines: 71,
72
(Zentralfriedhof,
Tor 2)

Clemens Holzmeister was awarded the contract to build the crematory although he only won third prize in the respective competition. Without knowing that his project was to be built in the garden of a "new" Renaissance Castle, he created a design that matched the site harmoniously. Holzmeister designed the original fortification-like structure close to the surrounding garden wall with the building's purpose in mind. The romantic-expressionist forms that were used on a Viennese community project for the first time here, became a model for community housing projects built later.

Behind the saw-like tooth-shaped boundary walls, Holzmeister seemingly embedded a cubic building within the structure that rises tower-like above the roof of the facility on four pillars which also act as chimneys. The building is concluded with a pyramid-shaped roof that is visible above the low walls. The effect of the pointy gothic arcade arches within form a broad square that is heightened by the pointy shape and dark, mysterious atmosphere of the entrance. This effect is developed to its fullest

KREMATORIUM

Clemens Holzmeister

extent in the hall of this "Cement Gothic" building.

The construction of the Viennese crematory gave the Austrian association of friends of cremation, "Die Flamme" (The Flame) the chance of making its maxim a reality: *"Lived as a proletarian, died as a proletarian and burned to ashes in the name of cultural progress!"*

VERKEHRSBÜRO

Heinrich Schmid, Hermann Aichinger

The Österreichische Verkehrsbüro (Austrian Travel Office) was opened at the end of 1917, during WWI. After the war, larger rooms were necessary for the office to be able to meet rising demand. The Municipality of Vienna and the Commission for Transport Facilities negotiated a twenty-year lease for a plot of land opposite the Secession (Page 78). The building was constructed a quarter of a century after the Secession and its, *"rather stolid mansion-like architecture"* was considered a, *"retrograde manifesto"* by contemporaries (Friedrich Achleitner). Two Wagner pupils, Heinrich Schmid and Hermann Aichinger, were commissioned to build the offices and both went on to become successful community housing project architects.

The site is particularly challenging from an urban planning perspective due to the radial course of the surrounding streets. The plot was located on top of the underground City Rail tracks (today's subway route) (Page 74), and extends to the arched struts over the River Wien. This unusual position influenced the layout and architectural structure of the building. It was only possible to lay foundations

I.
Friedrichstraße 7

Sightseeing:
During opening hours

Transportation:
Subways: U1, U2, U4 (Karlsplatz)

VERKEHRSBÜRO

Heinrich Schmid, Hermann Aichinger

longitudinally since neither the roof of the City Rail tunnel nor the struts over the River Wien could carry any weight. However, the wing over the City Rail was built higher than the structures resting on brackets opposite the Secession (Page 78).

A foyer leads to the two-level service area on the inside. The pillars and walls feature partial wood paneling.

FUCHSENFELD-HOF

Heinrich Schmid, Hermann Aichinger

XII.

Längenfeldgasse 68/
Eichenstraße/
Aßmayergasse/
Malfattigasse/
Steinbauergasse

Sightseeing:
Public areas only
Transportation:
Streetcar line: 62,
Bus: 10A
(Flurschützstraße,
Längenfeldgasse)

The Fuchsenfeld-Hof project, next to Metzleins-taler-Hof on Margaretengürtel in the city's 5th dis-trict is one of Vienna's first socialist community housing projects. In both cases, the construction plans go back to WWI, since the company ori-ginally in charge could not finance construction due to the currency devaluation at the time.

The entire complex was built in three construction phases from 1922 to 1925. The Reismann-Hof across the way on Längenfeldgasse was built in the third phase. The Otto Wagner pupils, Hermann Aichinger and Heinrich Schmid, were contracted to plan the ca. 1,100 residential unit facility.

The first and oldest construction segment was planned in 1915 and is bordered by Längenfeld-

FUCHSENFELD-HOF

Heinrich Schmid, Hermann Aichinger

gasse, Murlingengasse, Aßmayergasse and Neuwall-gasse. The straight-edged blocks and the four large courtyards create an almost Biedermeier-like ground level. This first building already contains all the important post-WWI improvements introduced in Viennese community housing: no inner courts, no long stairways, no aisle windows, no hallway toilets and running water in the apartments. This was also the first project to include shared facilities (a central laundry room, children's recreational rooms with integrated playground areas, kiddie pools, educational workshops, a reading room, kindergarten and a bathing facility.)

The Reismann-Hof was built during the third construction phase and features polygonal and round courtyards in keeping with the large, curving streets in the area. The buildings are partly decorated with hyperbolic-expressive details.

HAUS RUFER
Adolf Loos

XIII.
Schließmann-
gasse II

Sightseeing:
None

Transportation:
Subway: U4
(Braunschweig-
gasse)

Haus Rufer is another example of a, *"clever mini-malist variant of a single-family house,"* similar to Haus Horner (Page 158) (August Sarnitz), which was built ten years earlier. Contrary to the latter, in which the outer walls function as supports, Loos developed a structural solution with only one central support column in the middle of the building. Thus the architect was able to build the house for the entrepreneur and sugar merchant Josef Rufer on a surface of only 10 x 10 meters.

From the outside, the freely distributed windows on the façade of the house give the visitor a sense of the house's complex spatial arrangement. At the same time, Loos exercised restraint by only inter-rupting the strictly cubic shape of the house with the loggia and terrace he cut into the main floor. Loos' application of a copy of the Parthenon Frieze

HAUS RUFER

Adolf Loos

on the street-side façade helped harmonize the overall impression.

In order to complete the building without compromising his strict layout, Loos required the drafting architects not only to layer the floors on top of one another, but also to give the individual rooms adequate height for their respective purposes. The resulting varying ceiling heights give the visitor the impression of a constant, sequential spatial increase that ultimately surrounds him as a complete unit.

In 1930, the Loos biographer and associate Heinrich Kulka wrote in praise of Haus Rufer: *"The visitor is astonished by the volume of space in what seems like a small house on the outside. Haus Rufer is a standard example of a house this size. Fundamental improvements aren't possible."*

HAUS ARNOLD
Lois Welzenbacher

XVIII.
Sternwarte-
straße 83

Sightseeing:
None

Transportation:
Streetcar line: 41
(Gersthof)

Lois Welzenbacher was born in Munich in 1889 and attended Munich Technical University. After WWI, he began to work as an architect in Innsbruck and Munich. His first buildings (the Settari and Baldauf houses) were constructed in Southern Tyrol (Northern Italy) between 1919/20. Their moving, flowing shapes were to have great influence on alpine architecture.

The house Welzenbacher built for Hermann Arnold in 1923/24 was the first building he completed in Vienna. The building's structure and details were Welzenbacher's reaction to the house's location in an exclusive residential area. Nothing about it is reminiscent of his alpine buildings. Impressed by the refinement of Viennese Biedermeier living, the architect created a villa with strictly symmetrical main facades that calls to mind the buildings of both Josef Hoffmann and Josef Plečnik.

"The layout shows a tight unity between the house and garden. The concave shape of the façade bonds with the rounded top corner of the triangular plot, making the villa an indivisible unit." (Gustav

HAUS ARNOLD

Lois Welzenbacher

Künstler) The only ornaments on the steel street façade is the central balcony with its simple grating. Four straight-edged, tapered columns support this structure. The "lowered" pillar capitals distort the Biedermeier effect (August Sarnitz). This distortion reminds the visitor of Plečnik's column derivations, while the overall impression is closer to that of Josef Hoffmann's Villa Knips (Page 194).

By placing the staircase along the width of the building on the inside, the architect created a counterpoint to the building's axis.

AMALIENBAD

Otto Nadel, Karl Schmalhofer

1923
1926

X.
Reumannplatz 9

Sightseeing:
Open
to the public

Transportation:
Subway: U1
(Reumannplatz)

The public swimming pool in Vienna's 10th district is named after the city councillor Amalie Pölzer. It is a stone manifest of the Social Democratic city government's (endeavors) of the 20's and 30's to raise public hygiene awareness. The increased architectural importance of the project also led to the construction of a pool and other aquatic facilities in addition to the bathing wing. The cube-within-a-cube structure reaches its culmination at the building's center and is crowned by a water column, whose clock indicates the hour and the "new time." Karl Stemolak created the oversized female stone sculptures on the façade. The structure's Roman bath-like layout with its "manifold bathing facilities," was designed for 1,300 visitors. The symmetrically structured block

1923
1926

conceals a complex, comprehensive set of spaces including an indoor competition pool (with a massive glass sliding roof) therapeutic baths, showers, hairdressers, a restaurant, drying rooms and a "Tröpferlbad" (rentable bathtubs).

The heart of the almost religious building is the basilica-shaped swimming area with bleachers, a ten-meter diving board and a two-story gallery with changing booths. The shower and warm-water pool areas feature particularly sumptuous ceramic tiling that shows the transition between late Secession style and Art Déco in Viennese crafts.

Erich Schlöss and Erich Millbacher completed a general renovation of the building (between 1979 and 1986) paying careful attention to the preservation of historical elements.

VILLA KNIPS
Josef Hoffmann

XIX.
Nusswaldgasse 22

Sightseeing:
None

Transportation:
Streetcar line: 37
(Barawitzka-
gasse)

The Knips villa – whose owner Sonja Knips was portrayed by Gustav Klimt – is the last large town-house built by Josef Hoffmann. As opposed to Villa Skywa-Primavesi (Page 168), which consisted of many cubes, the architect chose a more tightly composed structure for this project that was influenced by the privacy of Viennese Biedermeier style.

On the exterior, the house is clearly divided between residential and public areas. However, Hoffmann concentrated on the individual façades to create this separation, instead of the respective rooms' volume. The fronts appear to be thin, almost immaterial surfaces united at the edges of the building. This design can be traced back to his teacher, Otto Wagner (see Wagner's apartment building at Neustiftgasse 40 (Page 142)), as well as the small diamond-shaped ornaments on the façades. It can be plainly seen that the elements that still insinuated function on Wagner's Postsparkasse (Page 110)

VILLA KNIPS

Josef Hoffmann

1924
1925

or on the Kirche Am Steinhof (Page 118) are pure-ly decorative on this project.

The garden side is more densely structured than the street side of the house. However, the narrow building only offers enough depth for two room layers. The visitor is guided from the foyer to the large salon; followed by the dining room and guest rooms. The living area, dining room, kitchen and pantry are divided by double-sided, room-high closets that bear testament to Hoffmann's desire to create complete design solutions. A hallway leads to the service area that includes a staircase for house personnel. Hoffman also planned additional living rooms and bedrooms (with bathrooms) for the first floor and attic, as well as a library.

WIEDENHOFER-HOF

Josef Frank

XVII.
Zeillergasse 7–11/
Beringgasse 15/
Liebknecht-
gasse 10–12/
Pretschgogasse 5

Sightseeing:
Public areas only

Transportation:
Streetcar line: 43
(Hernals)

Josef Frank was a proponent of single-family housing (*"It cannot be stressed often enough that the
single-family house is the foundation of our entire
modern building technology and of our urban facilities."*) He wrote essays and spoke against the
"People's Apartment Palaces" that had been erected by the Viennese city council all over Vienna
during the twenties and thirties. But Frank was
nonetheless forced to submit to the constraints of
his contractors since he did want to participate in
Viennese construction projects. However, Frank's
housing projects show a desire to separate themselves from the pathetic "superblocks" of the time.
The city's authorities ignored his demand for low
construction density in his preliminary plans for

WIEDENHOFER-HOF
Josef Frank

the Wiedenhofer-Hof project on Kongressplatz and building in the area reached an almost unacceptable density level for Frank. Despite having to build right up to the edge of the block, Frank nonetheless managed to realize his, *"visions of scale, a variety of forms and clarity"* (August Sarnitz), on the façade facing Kongresspark. The building's structure is loosened by the generously sized loggias on its dividing edges. The middle wing extensions create a tongue-like division between the two courtyards. The pronounced slope of the site made it necessary to link both of these open spaces with a wide staircase but Frank was nonetheless able to construct all the buildings with their eaves at a single level despite their differing sizes.

The building's unusual, deep orange-red hue contrasted with the white window surfaces, which encouraged the Viennese to name the complex the "Paprikahof."

The expansion in 1953, the hall window additions and the elevator shafts added later disturb the project's well-balanced proportions.

SANDLEITEN-HOF
Hoppe & Schönthal & Matouschek,
Theiss & Jaksch, Krauss & Tölk

Sandleiten-
gasse 43–51 /
Steinmüllergasse /
Mietschlgasse /
Baumeistergasse

Sightseeing:
Public areas only

Transportation:
Streetcar line: 44
(Sandleitengasse)

The housing project non pareil: with 1576 apartments, the Sandleitenhof project was the largest
single complex to be approved by the Social Democratic Vienna City Council as part of the drive
to build 25,000 residential units in 1923. A large
team of architects was assembled that can only be
compared to the work group entrusted with the
construction of the Winarsky-Hof (Page 200).
While that group included Peter Behrens, Josef
Frank, Oskar Strnad and many others who took
their architectural cues from international projects,
the Sandleiten-Hof team consisted of architects
who took a more homegrown approach. Hence
the differences between the two complexes can already be recognized in their differing ground
plans: the Winarsky-Hof is a contained block structure, whereas the Sandleiten-Hof's construction
pattern follows the romantic, steep incline of the
site, creating an ensemble of squares and courtyards. The building's structural features change
constantly when viewed from South to North, although these variations are imperceptible to passersby. The design is initially defined by ribbon-like

square enclosures (Hoppe/Schönthal/Matouschek)
that gradually evolve into open structures (Theiss/
Jaksch und Krauss/Tölk) as the project premises
reach the borders of the exclusive residential area
at the other end.

Although Otto Wagner's pupils Hoppe, Schönthal
and Matouschek were involved in designing the
complex, it mainly follows the concept set down
by his rival (in terms of urban onstruction),
Camillo Sitte.

The three teams of architects had been selected in
a competition for which seven teams were asked
to draft proposals.

The kindergarten facility on the Sandleitengasse
end of the project is particularly noteworthy. It was
built by the city official Erich Franz Leischner in
accordance with the teachings of Maria Montessori.

WINARSKY-HOF
Behrens, Dirnhuber, Frank, Hoffmann, Lihotzky, Schuster, Strnad, Wlach et al.

XX.
Stromstraße
36–38 /
Winarskystraße /
Durchlaufstraße /
Pasettistraße

Sightseeing:
None

Transportation:
Subway: U6
(Dresdner Straße)

The Austrian Housing and Small Garden Association entrusted its five staff architects as well as Grete Lihotzky, Franz Schuster and Oskar Wlach with the design of three housing units containing around 700 apartments on an almost perfect rectangle bordered by Strom-, Vorgarten-, Winarsky- und Pasettistraße. Karl Dirnhuber joined the group, which was considered the elite of Viennese architecture at the time.

When planning was already underway, it was decided that the site would be extended to include a triangular plot of land on Durchlaufstraße, the street to the south of the projected building. Adolf

WINARSKY-HOF
Behrens, Dirnhuber, Frank, Hoffmann, Lihotzky,
Schuster, Strnad, Wlach et al.

1924
1925

Loos had planned a terraced building for the site, but it was not built. Grete Lihotzky was ultimately responsible for the site and this segment of the complex was named "Otto-Haas-Hof".

The team developed a "courtyard within a courtyard" approach to the "Winarsky-Hof", which was built symmetrically along the axis of Leystraße. The outer blocks included a public school and the Brigitta Hospital. The 534-apartment complex includes studios, a bathing facility, library, commercial locales, a kindergarten, halls and workshops.

The fact that each wing reflects the individual artistic personality of the architect who built it offers the visitor the opportunity to make direct comparisons. However, the freedom of design the architects enjoyed was detrimental to the entire complex: the building front facing Winarskystraße is the work of three different architects!

REUMANN-HOF
Hubert Gessner

V.
Margaretengürtel
100 – 110 /
Brandmayer-
gasse 37 – 39 /
Siebenbrunnen-
gasse 90 – 92

Sightseeing:
Public areas only

Transportation:
Streetcar lines: 6,
18 (Eichenstraße)

The international high rise competitions for the Chicago Tribune and Friedrichstraße in Berlin led to a high rise polemic in Vienna. As a result, Hubert Gessner included a 12-story ca. 40 meter-high building flanked by two courtyards in his preliminary draft. However, the high rise lacked the expressive folds of the mid-sized building ultimately constructed on the site, The initial plan was to devise a street layout that that would divide the project into individual blocks, but this plan was abandoned in favor of overall architectural uniformity.

The completion of this project was hampered by a series of unprofessionally led debates and polemics. The main building was finally built with fewer floors than originally planned, creating a complex in which the central wing and lateral wings seemingly merge to create a single unit. Thus the project was given a castle-like appearance with the respective attributes: a ceremonial court, arcades, as well as a main and latitudinal axis. The links to feudal architecture and palace construction weren't merely the result of a thwarted design. They were

REUMANN-HOF

Hubert Gessner

also rooted in a series of architectural details that affected the entire facility. One of these features was the dominating ceremonial court in front of the elevated central building. The street end of the square is blocked off by purely decorative deciduous tree-lined walkways with pavilions that remind the visitor of gatekeeper's booths. Another feudal architecture element was the water basin, which was intended to offer a reflection of the castle, i.e. the main building. Gessner's palace-like grounds plan for the Reumann-Hof became the standard "Superblock" design and a blueprint for all community housing complexes built on this scale by the City of Vienna.

The building was one of the main bases of the "Republikanischer Schutzbund" (Republican Protection Union) in 1934.

RABEN-HOF

Heinrich Schmid, Hermann Aichinger

III.

Baumgasse 29–41/
Rabengasse 1–9 &
2–12/ Hainburger
Straße 68–70/
Kardinal-Nagl
-Platz 5

Sightseeing:
Public areas only

Transportation:
Subway: U3
(Kardinal-Nagl-
Platz)

The complex is located on the former Krimsky barracks' grounds and its 1,100 units make it one of the largest Socialist community housing projects in Vienna. The project features a kindergarten, public library and a central laundry as well as a remarkable foyer that was adapted as a theater in 1990.

The architects Heinrich Schmid and Hermann Aichinger, who completed many projects for the Social Democratic Vienna city administration during the first republic, were forced to build the project in stages. The reasons for this were: the numerous mandatory requirements such as the use of the fire protection walls of existing older buildings and the need to integrate the trajectory of important connecting streets in the complex's de-sign. Another hindrance was the fact that the necessary sites still had to be purchased after the project was approved. This made it impossible to build the facility with an axial orientation right from the start. Although Wagner had trained the architects to build "Superblocks," they chose to create long, ribbon-like building sequences with open courts.

One of the complex's design highlights was the integration of Rabengasse, which curves through the entire facility. Major differences between the individual structures, both in terms of height and with respect to the materials used, are characteri-stic of the Raben-Hof project. The New Gothic Renaissance features such as the pointy arches and brick paneling are closely related to the Northern European Expressionism of Hans Poelzig or Fritz Höger and the "Amsterdam School."

Heinrich Schmid and Hermann Aichinger's achie-vement was the creation of a logical, cohesive unit, despite the myriad of differing elements listed above.

VOGELWEID-HOF ("MÄRCHEN-HOF")
Leopold Bauer

XV

Hütteldorfer
Straße 2A /
Wurzbachgasse 2/
Sorbaitgasse 3

Sightseeing:
Public areas only

Transportation:
Subway: U6
(Burggasse)

Leopold Bauer, who was from Silesia, as was Joseph Maria Olbrich, succeeded Otto Wagner at the Academy of Fine Arts (Page 42) in 1913 despite resistance from the student body. This resistance arose from Bauer's criticism of Wagner's rationalism as of 1906. In 1919, Bauer asked to be replaced as a result of the increasing rift between him and his students. From then on, he pursued a Historicist approach under the motto, "Tradition, not imitation," although this style had been condemned by Wagner and his disciples.

Although he was the founder of a middle-class bourgeois political party and openly opposed the Social Democratic Party in essays, he nonetheless participated in Socialist community housing pro-

VOGELWEID-HOF ("MÄRCHEN-HOF")

Leopold Bauer

1926
1927

jects and defended their large-scale complexes. The architect solved the problems posed by the relatively narrow plot of land by extending construction over the sidewalk and designing a covered, tree-lined walkway that gave him enough space to build an appropriately monumental residential building featuring the required depth and a respectably sized courtyard. In accordance with his demand that the state and City of Vienna support the fine arts by commissioning monumental arts-related projects in order to educate the public, he designed the tree-lined walkway as a form of open-air museum with murals and ceiling paintings by Rudolf Jettmar and Franz Wacik. These include four idealized depictions of pre-industrial crafts and six scenes from famous fables. These decorations led to the building's designation as the "Märchen-Hof" (Fairytale Court). The rows of grooved circular arches and the unique, projecting ledges of the middle building show the architect's romantic playfulness. The ceramic fountains in the courtyard are the work of Robert Obsieger.

PALAIS WITTGENSTEIN
(today: Bulgarian Cultural Institute)

1926
1928

Paul Engelmann, Ludwig Wittgenstein

III.
Kundmanngasse 19

Sightseeing:
By appointment

Transportation:
Subway: U3
(Rochusgasse)

Until its "discovery" at the end of the sixties/ beginning of the seventies, the few interested passersby that happened to walk down Kundmanngasse were always reminded of Adolf Loos's work when they saw the building there.

This building is a unique example of architecture of particular historical importance to the field. It isn't only important as a building, its significance is also related to the persons who were directly or indirectly involved in its construction. The versatile, talented Loos pupil and friend of Ludwig Wittgenstein, Paul Engelmann, developed the rough architectural concept of the building. Wittgenstein, who was probably the most important philosopher of the 20th century, took Engelmann's design a step further and gave the structure its unmistakable character, defined by the

PALAIS WITTGENSTEIN

(today: Bulgarian Cultural Institute)

Paul Engelmann, Ludwig Wittgenstein

1926
1928

clever proportions, the radical reduction of the construction materials used (iron, glass, cement and marble stucco) and the purist cube-within-a-cube exterior structure. The contractor, Margaret Stonborough-Wittgenstein, was Wittgenstein's sister and a Viennese socialite, who is still remembered today due to Gustav Klimt's portrait of her. The siblings were the children of the extremely wealthy steel magnate Karl Wittgenstein.

The attempt was made time and again to find parallels between architecture and Wittgenstein's philosophical work by citing the "Tractatus logico-philosophicus," Wittgenstein's main work, published in 1919. However, the building's biographer, Paul Wijdeveld, proved that Wittgenstein did not consider the house a symbol of his philosophical teachings.

KARL-MARX-HOF
Karl Ehn

1926
1930

XIX.
Heiligenstädter
Straße /
Grinzinger Straße /
Boschstraße

Sightseeing:
Public areas only

Transportation:
Subway: U4
(Heiligenstadt)

With its 1,300 residential units the Karl-Marx-Hof isn't the largest "Red" Viennese housing project (Sandleiten-Hof [Page 198] has 1,500 apartments), but it is certainly the most famous. The complex, which was fittingly called, "a kilometer of Art Déco," was built on a narrow patch of meadowland between Heiligenstädterstraße and the tracks of the Franz-Josephs-Bahn railway. The construction of a "Superblock" here was meant to bring Social Democratic voters into a predominantly Christian Socialist district.

The Wagner pupil and Viennese construction authorities employee Karl Ehn's design won the competition for which Clemens Holzmeister also submitted a proposal. By placing the complex's buildings along the borders of the site, Ehn was able to create enormous garden-like courtyards that also contained the shared facilities. Thus Ehn only built on 18% of the total available surface. He designed the central building as a form of ceremonial edifice whose six towers rise above the broad

KARL-MARX-HOF

Karl Ehn

arches. These arches were intended to welcome the returning masses of workers to their homes.

Josef Riedel's ceramic sculptures on the façade of the middle building depict "Freedom," "Care," "Enlightenment," and "Body Culture." The bronze "Sower" statue at the center of the courtyard was modeled by Otto Hofner.

The martial overall impression of the building led the Austrian Fascists to consider the Karl-Marx-Hof the "Red Fortress" and open fire on it during the political disturbances of 1934.

The importance of the building's coloring in giving the massive buildings a sense of lightness became clear during the recent general renovation supervised by Franz Kiener.

KARL-SEITZ-HOF
Hubert Gessner

XXI.
Jedleseer
Straße 66–94 /
Voltagasse 20–38 /
Bunsengasse 1–3 /
Dunantgasse 1–15 /
Edisongasse

Sightseeing:
Public areas only

Transportation:
Streetcar line: 26
(Koloniestraße)

In 1925, the City of Vienna intended to build residential units on a number of sites throughout the city. However, due to economic considerations, it was decided that one complex should be built on one large plot of land. A competition for such a project was announced in late autumn 1925, was restricted to entries by Karl Krist, Robert Örley and Hubert Gessner, and was won by Hubert Gessner.

Since the 25,000th apartment of the Viennese community housing program announced in 1923 would be completed as part of the "Gartenstadt" (Garden City) complex, the festivities surrounding the placement of the cornerstone on June 29th 1926 were particularly impressive. Federal President

KARL-SEITZ-HOF
Hubert Gessner

Dr. Michael Hainisch, as well as the Mayor and the usual collection of city Councillors, attended the ceremony.

Gessner explained the new form of Garden City he had created in Jedlesee in an extensive newspaper interview: *"It was my intention to create a transition to the form of building that I find most worth striving for: garden-city-like construction. I would like to note that my concept of a garden city is totally different to the common notion. It doesn't mean that each house should have a garden in front of it. Instead, the houses themselves should be located in a park."*

The most impressive segment of Gartenstadt Jedlesee is the monumental exedra with its lateral clock tower and axial portal. These are the facility's design highlights. The tower featured the first elevator to be installed in a Viennese community housing project.

In 1945, "Gartenstadt Jedlesee" was unofficially christened "Karl-Seitz-Hof." This became the official name after Karl Seitz's death in 1950.

HAUS MOLLER
Adolf Loos

XVIII.
Starkfriedgasse 19

Sightseeing:
None

Transportation:
Streetcar line: 41
(Scheibenberg-
straße)

Adolf Loos left Vienna once and for all in 1924, after a number of disappointments. He went to France hoping to receive appealing contracts there and remained until 1928. He was in Paris when his friends Hans and Anny Moller hired him to build their villa in the spring of 1927. As a result, his associate Jacques Groag supervised the construction of Villa Moller in Vienna. Hans Moller was an engineer, textile manufacturer and the owner of

HAUS MOLLER

Adolf Loos

the company S. Katzau in Babí u Nachod and the chairman of the "Friends of Adolf Loos" committee.

Villa Moller fits seamlessly among the Loos buildings built during his period in France. The architect created a strictly symmetrical "public" street front that contrasts with the more loosely conceived "private" garden façade. Thus the house is a departure from his earlier designs such as Haus Strasser (Page 180), where there is no difference between the two façades. On the other hand, Loos used the exterior walls as supports on Haus Moller, just as he had done with Haus Horner (Page 158), which was built on a small budget. This design facilitated the integration of the house's rooms with one another. It was also contrary to the Haus Rufer (Page 188) arrangement in which he used a central supportive column.

The cube-shaped structure was built on a 25 x 21 meter surface with a terrace projecting from the upper portion of the ground floor and a partially developed upper level, which gives the building the appearance of a terraced house.

The interior boasts a number of sophisticated solutions, such as the elevated dining area (this made it possible to use it as a music podium) with collapsible stairs, making the house a highly interesting sample of Loos' work.

GEORGE-WASHINGTON-HOF
Karl Krist, Robert Örley

X.
Wienerbergstraße /
Untere Meidlinger
Straße /
Kastanienallee

Sightseeing:
Public areas only

Transportation:
Streetcar line: 65
(Windtenstraße)

In late autumn 1925, the City of Vienna announced a competition that was restricted to entries by
Robert Örley, Karl Krist and Hubert Gessner for
the proposed Gartenstadt Jedlesee (today's Karl-
Seitz-Hof [Page 212]). Örley presented five designs, but Gessner won and was awarded the contract. As compensation, Krist and Örley were assigned to plan another Garden City barely a year later
in 1926, before the Urban Construction Conference held in Vienna that year. The project was
the "Wohnhausanlage Am Wienerberg – Spinnerin
am Kreuz," which was later renamed the "George-
Washington-Hof."

The complex was built on the former grounds of
the "Bürgerspitalfond" (Citizen's Hospital Fund)
and is one of the largest of its kind. Although it can
be considered a "Superblock" in typological terms,
this building type's characteristic pathos was diluted with "small town" details such as gates, little
towers and oriel rooms as well as its somewhat looser structuring on the outer edges. The looser
structure may have been a consequence of the

GEORGE-WASHINGTON-HOF
Karl Krist, Robert Örley

1927
1930

criticism that was voiced with respect to the large complexes built until the 1926 Urban Construction Conference held in Vienna that year.

The groups of buildings are arranged around courtyards and were named after the types of trees planted in the project. The more enclosed segment of the complex (Ulmen- and Akazienhof on Wienerbergerstrasse) was designed by Örley, whereas the more loosely structured parts on the corner of Wienerbergerstrasse and Triesterstraße are the work of Krist.

This complex also featured the shared facilities that were common to all large-scale Viennese community housing projects: a number of commercial locales, a library and a mothercare counseling office as well as baths and a laundry room.

KONGRESSBAD

Erich Franz Leischner

XVI.
Kongressplatz

Sightseeing:
During opening
hours

Transportation:
Streetcar line: 43
(Hernals)

The two outstanding Vienna Construction Authority's staff architects between the two wars were
the Wagner pupil Karl Ehn and Erich Franz
Leischner, who studied under Carl König at the
Vienna Technical University. Both were responsible
for the construction of major projects in Vienna.
Among Leischner's many duties were the supervision of the waterworks, schools, electricity plants
and the architecture department. As a freelance architect, he left a remarkable architectural legacy,
both in terms of quality and quantity.

The Kongressbad public swimming pool was built
as one of the supplemental measures stipulated by
the City of Vienna's community housing project
program enacted during the two World Wars. In
architectural terms it is one of the city's most interesting "Sommer-, Schwimm-, Luft- und Sonnen-
bäder" (summertime swimming-, air- and sun-
baths) facilities. It is also part of one of Vienna's
most important urban construction projects of

KONGRESSBAD

Erich Franz Leischner

the post-WWI era, Sandleiten-Hof (Page 198) (Leischner built the project's kindergarten). Other major housing projects include Wiedenhofer-Hof (Page 196) (Josef Frank), the Kongresspark with its dairy and bistro (both by Leischner) and the open-air children's pool (also by Leischner). The "booth and Prater amusement park-style architecture" of the elongated slightly curved entrance with its red-white-red (the city colors) wood planking is a departure from the usual pathos of the period's community projects and a symbol of the Viennese worker movement's fundamentally sober attitude. The structure's central, elevated portal, the striking flagpoles mounted in the façade's poured concrete front, the long lateral wings and the corner pavilions represent Leischner's adaptation of castle architecture to the needs of the proletariat.

UMSPANNWERK
Eugen Kastner, Fritz Waage

X.
Humboldt-
gasse 1–5

Sightseeing:
None

Transportation:
Subway: U1
(Südtiroler Platz)

Fritz Waage, who was born in 1898 and trained at the Vienna Technical University, had been an associate of Hubert Gessner's before he formed a working partnership with Eugen Kastner. He and other Gessner associates designed the Lassalle-Hof (1924). After completing the transformer station, Kastner and Waage built the two remarkable buildings for the Dorotheum auction house in Währing, Vienna's 18th district (Gentzgasse, 1931) and in Floridsdorf (21st district, Pitkagasse, 1934).

Their transformer station in Favoriten (the 10th district) is one the most impressive structures built in Vienna between the two wars, and its style remains unmatched. The inconvenient triangular construction site forced the architects to integrate

UMSPANNWERK

Eugen Kastner, Fritz Waage

the technical and administrative areas of this challenging project in a, *"linear motion and addition plan"* (Friedrich Achleitner). The architects explained the parameters of the assignment in a description of the project: *"The individual rooms had to be built to meet very strict height and width specifications since it was mandatory to place the machines either next to or on top of one another... Achieving this was hampered by the triangular shape of the plot since a logical room order was required from a technical point of view. This was necessary to allow for a logical arrangement of the respective machinery, short connecting halls, quick access to the most important operational rooms, and short power lines etc."* The building was built in a less densely populated area using silo and steamer motifs. The plinth-like ground level gives the building a sculpted appearance.

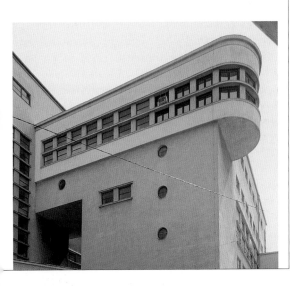

AUGARTENBRÜCKE
Hubert Gessner

In 1782, the third bridge – after the Schweden-
and Franzensbrücke – was built across the Danube
Canal at the request of Kaiser Joseph II. This was
the first Augartenbrücke. The wooden bridge was
burned down by the French in 1809 and replaced
again by a wood structure. A steel chain bridge was
built on the site in 1872 that was named after
Empress Maria Theresia. Although the bridge was
initially only supposed to be reinforced to meet the
demands of increasing traffic in 1927, the decision
was made to build a new bridge on the site in
1928. A competition was announced the same year
and 23 designs were submitted. Five of the proposals suggested a ferroconcrete solution for the
task. However, the decision was ultimately made in
favor of a 75-meter- long, 16 meter-wide-iron
suspension bridge built by the Waagner-Biro A. G.
bridge building company according to a design by
Hubert Gessner.

Work began with great care. Precision during construction became so important that the granite
blocks used on both banks were inspected with
microscopes to be certain they met the required
quality standards.

The pronounced, projecting sidewalk slabs that

II. und IX.
Untere
Augartenstraße /
Franz-Josef-Kai /
Donaukanal

Sightseeing:
Open
to the public

Transportation:
Subways: U2, U4
(Schottenring)

AUGARTENBRÜCKE

Hubert Gessner

1928
1931

widen as one reaches the other side guide pedestrians to the bridge, enticing them to cross it. The sightseeing platforms on the bridgeheads invite visitors to stay a bit longer before using the granite steps that lead to the promenade on the bank.

The inaugural speech read as follows: *"the beauty of a bridge is guaranteed by the interplay of strength resulting from the structure's design,"* making any form of ornamentation superfluous. Gessner chose curiously shaped pylons for the bridge's lighting in order to stress the convergence of architecture and technology.

HAUS BEER
Josef Frank, Oskar Wlach

XIII.
Wenzgasse 12

Sightseeing:
None

Transportation:
Streetcar line: 60
(Gloriettegasse)

The house built by Julius Beer and Josef Frank with the cooperation of Oskar Wlach encourages comparisons, especially with the single-family houses built by Adolf Loos, one of which is in the immediate vicinity (Haus Scheu [Page 164]). Frank developed the Loosian "spatial plan" a step further in his project. The house is easily accessible as a consequence of the freer room sequence (compared to Loos' houses), which can be recognized as *"pockets of space"* (Josef Frank). *"A well-organized house should be designed like a city, with streets and paths that inevitably lead to places..."* (Josef Frank) and the split-level arrangement of the hall and living room floors creates a spatial *"backbone"* (Friedrich Achleitner). The closed street façade contrasts with the garden façade, which features a number of window openings and balconies on brackets that integrates the garden with the interior as opposed to Loos' precepts.

In the article Frank published when the house was completed "Das Haus als Weg und Platz", for which Haus Beer is a built manifesto, he propagated a departure from what was (to him) useless uniformity . Hence the house is free of the brittle

HAUS BEER
Josef Frank, Oskar Wlach

Classicism detectable in Loos' work. Frank's decision to do without built in furniture created a "mobile" interior and made a fixed room distribution unnecessary. The architect only adhered to a strict spatial system in terms of the walls' proportions, for which he used a series of squares and derivatives thereof.

By blending rules with freedom and incorporating Anglo-Saxon and Far Eastern influences, Frank created a masterpiece that can be considered, *"a major example of new Viennese living."*

WOHNHAUSANLAGE
FRIEDRICH-ENGELS-PLATZ

Rudolf Perco

XX.
Friedrich-Engels-
Platz /
Wehlistraße /
Leystraße /
Forsthausgasse /
Kapaunplatz

Sightseeing:
Public areas only

Transportation:
Streetcar line: 31
(Friedrich-Engels-
Platz)

Although Engelsplatz-Hof's 1,467 apartments make it only insignificantly smaller than Sandleiten-Hof (Page 198), it is the far more monumental project. It is the antithesis of the loose "Super-block" design of both the Sandleiten-Hof (Page 198) and Raben-Hof (Page 204). Its monumentality and cross-axiality correspond to Otto Wagner's (Rudolf Perco's teacher) vision of an "Ideal plan for the expansion of the 22nd district", which is reflected in his "Artibus" study. Perco reduced and simplified the details in favor of the structure's large shape, which is designed for best effect at a distance. The Wagner-like rationalism can be re-

WOHNHAUSANLAGE
FRIEDRICH-ENGELS-PLATZ
Rudolf Perco

cognized in the sequence of cube-shaped blocks, the façades' structure and the monotonous arrangement of solid masses and ledges. These elements are only interrupted in certain areas, such as the entrance area, which reflects the architect's craze for things big, as well as the eight-story residential towers, the constructivist balcony clusters and the huge, exaggerated flagpoles.

The rectangular Kapaunplatz square is the center of the facility. It intersects the complex's two main axes and gives the entire project, which was built on an uneven plot a clear sense of order. The structure's other defining feature is the construction of its buildings along the edge of the site.

The laundry and bathing facilities contrast with the academic symmetry and design of the complex's details. Perco *"played a stylistically pleasing game with both cubic and dynamic shapes"* (Helmut Weihsmann). The proportions, asymmetry and expressionist brick paneling of the clock tower are examples of outstanding plotting and design.

WERKBUNDSIEDLUNG
J. Frank, G. Rietveld, J. Hoffmann, A. Loos,
H. Kulka, A. Lurçat, E. A. Plischke, H. Häring et al.

1930
1932

XIII.
Jagdschlossgasse /
Veitingergasse /
Woinovichgasse /
Jagicgasse

Sightseeing:
Public areas only

Transportation:
Bus: 54B
(Gobergasse)

Josef Frank was the only Austrian who participated in the construction of the Weissenhof project in Stuttgart, Germany (1927). Frank had two reasons for pursuing the construction of the Wiener Werkbundsiedlung project: one was his criticism of the monumental complexes built in "red" Vienna and the other was the possibility of presenting an alternative to the Stuttgart project. However, Frank's goal was to explore the manifold possibilities in the field of spatial and functional solutions, whereas the German project emphasized new building technologies and a new construction style. The idea was to present single- and multi-family houses, as well as terraced houses of different types and in different sizes (60–100 m²). Frank didn't only succeed in persuading the young avantgarde of Austrian architects. He also convinced his old Werkbund adversaries Loos und Hoffmann and the circle of architects close to Clemens Holzmeister to participate. Frank also invited the international greats he thought had been ignored in the Stuttgart project. The three expatriates, Richard Neutra, Arthur Grünberger and Grete Schütte-Lihotzky also participated in the project.

WERKBUNDSIEDLUNG
J. Frank, G. Rietveld, J. Hoffmann, A. Loos,
H. Kulka, A. Lurçat, E. A. Plischke, H. Häring et al.

1930
1932

WERKBUNDSIEDLUNG
J. Frank, G. Rietveld, J. Hoffmann, A. Loos,
H. Kulka, A. Lurçat, E. A. Plischke, H. Häring et al.

Since the site was located on a damp meadow, it was necessary to build cellars, although the original plan had been to build low-cost housing. The color concept created by the Hungarian painter Lazlo Gabor sets the building apartment from the white structures of the pure "International Style."
Despite the planned "coincidences" that result from the twisting paths and seemingly natural open spaces, the complex still seems to be more of an exhibition than an actual housing project. The 70 houses and their model furniture were opened to the public in the summer of 1932 as part of an exhibition.
Adolf Krischanitz and Otto Kapfinger renovated the complex in 1983–85.

Veitingergasse

71, 73 Hugo Häring, Berlin
75, 77 Richard Bauer, Vienna
79, 81, 83, 85 Josef Hoffmann, Vienna
87, 89, 91, 93 André Lurçat, Paris
95, 97 Walter Sobotka, Vienna
(destroyed in 1945)
99, 101 Oskar Wlach, Vienna
103, 105 Julius Jirasek, Vienna
107, 109 Ernst A. Plischke, Vienna
111, 113 Josef Wenzel, Vienna
115, 117 Oswald Haerdtl, Vienna

Jagdschlossgasse

68, 70 Helmut Wagner-Freynsheim, Vienna
72, 74 Otto Breuer, Vienna
76, 78 Josef F. Dex, Vienna
80, 82 Arthur Grünberger, Vienna
88, 90 Ernst Lichtblau, Vienna

XIII.
Jagdschlossgasse /
Veitingergasse /
Woinovichgasse /
Jagicgasse

Sightseeing:
Public areas only

Transportation:
Bus: 54B
(Gobergasse)

WERKBUNDSIEDLUNG

J. Frank, G. Rietveld, J. Hoffmann, A. Loos,
H. Kulka, A. Lurçat, E. A. Plischke, H. Häring et al.

Woinovichgasse

2, 4   Margarete Schütte-Lihotzky, Moscow
6, 8   Max Fellerer, Vienna
1, 3   Hugo Gorge, Vienna
5, 7   Jacques Groag, Paris
9   Richard Neutra, Los Angeles
11   Hans Adolf Vetter, Vienna
13, 15, 17, 19   Adolf Loos,
                 Heinrich Kulka Vienna
10, 12   Gabriel Guévrékian, Paris
14, 16, 18, 20   Gerrit Thomas Rietveld,
                 Utrecht
22   Eugen Wachberger, Vienna
24, 26   Walter Loos, Vienna
28, 30   Karl Anton Bieber,
         Otto Niedermoser, Vienna
32   Josef Frank, Vienna
34   Hugo Häring, Berlin

Jagicgasse

8, 10   Clemens Holzmeister, Vienna
12   Eugen Wachberger, Vienna

Engelbrechtweg

4, 6   Hugo Häring, Berlin
(destroyed in 1945)
5, 7   Oskar Strnad, Vienna
(destroyed in 1945)
9, 11   Anton Brenner, Vienna

HOCHHAUS HERRENGASSE
Siegfried Theiss, Hans Jaksch

I.
Herrengasse 6–8/
Fahnengasse 2/
Wallnerstraße 5–7

Sightseeing:
None

Transportation:
Subway: U3
(Herrengasse)

The cooperation between Siegfried Theiss and Hans Jaksch began in the years preceding WWI and only ended around 1960. One of the indisputable highlights (in every sense) of their long cooperation was the Herrengasse high rise, although the use of that term for the building remains controversial to this day.

The debate on whether to build a high rise in Vienna or not had already begun in the mid-twenties. The Socialist city administration had already been close to building a high rise on the grounds of the charitable institution at the Währinger Straße/Spitalgasse corner site. Theiss & Jaksch participated in the competition of this project, but the Wagner pupil Rudolf Frass won it. However, the

HOCHHAUS HERRENGASSE

Siegfried Theiss, Hans Jaksch

project was never built since the Christian Socialist federal government introduced new tax legislation that effectively eliminated the project's funding.

A year later, the "Creditinstitut für öffentliche Unternehmungen," (Credit Institute for Public Enterprises) decided to build a high rise on a site in Vienna's inner city. Theiss & Jaksch designed a 16-story building built to the edges of the plot and featuring a steel structural skeleton, for the site on the corner of Fahnengasse and Herrengasse. The building tapers inwards step-by-step from the 12th floor upwards. The two-story glass superstructure was (formerly) used as a coffeehouse.

The reduced amount of shapes and the almost completely uniform design of the façade is nearly devoid of modernistic details. The black glass paneling creates a plinth zone consisting of commercial locales and offices. The structure contains 120 family units and 150 "bachelor pads." The linking up of the building with the neighboring Looshaus (Page 146) was carried out with great care.

ARBEITSAMT LIESING
Ernst A. Plischke

The then new assignment of building an "Arbeits-amt" (employment office) was symptomatic for the economically difficult twenties. This triggered a search for functionally appropriate solutions in some cities. Walter Gropius built a circular employ-ment office in Dessau in 1928/29. In Vienna, Hermann Stiegholzer and Herbert Kastinger built the construction industry employment office in Ottakring (the 16th district) in 1926/27 and the metal and wood industry employment office in the 5th district as block-like, monumental structures.

Plischke, was born in Klosterneuburg (right out-side Vienna) in 1903 and initially trained under Oskar Strnad at the Viennese Art Trade School before continuing his studies under Peter Behrens at the Academy of Fine Arts (Page 42). He had been to the United States before being awarded the contract to build the Arbeitsamt Liesing in 1929/30. Hence he tried to adapt the knowledge he had acquired in New York to conditions in Austria and and apply it to "his" employment offi-ce. As a result, he created a unique, uncompromi-

XXIII.
Dr.-Neumann-Gasse 7

Sightseeing:
None

Transportation:
Bus: 60A
(Dr.-Neumann-Gasse)

ARBEITSAMT LIESING

Ernst A. Plischke

sing building with impressively plastic features in the "International Style."

The large, street-side opening with its continuous row of windows, which reveal the round support elements was only possible due to the ferroconcrete skeleton structure of the building. The effect was considered spectacular at the time. The use of glass in the stairwell at the front of the building heightens the effect, creating the impression of complete "transparency". This programmatic lucidness was contrasted by the closed garden-side front. *"The office's characteristic as a public building is unmistakably visible through the glass wall. There are no secrets hidden behind less-than-transparent counter separations. "* (Ernst A. Plischke)

LITERATURE

Friedrich Achleitner, *Österreichische Architektur im 20. Jahrhundert*, Vol. III/1, Wien: 1.–12. Bezirk, Salzburg-Wien 1990

Friedrich Achleitner, *Österreichische Architektur im 20. Jahrhundert*, Vol. III/2, Wien: 13.–18. Bezirk, Salzburg-Wien 1995

Josef Engelhart, *Ein Wiener Maler erzählt. Mein Leben und meine Modelle*, Wien 1943

Josef Frank, *Das Haus als Weg und Platz*, in: Baumeister, 29. Jg., Wien 1931, S. 316

Otto Antonia Graf, *Otto Wagner. 1. Das Werk des Architekten. 1860–1902*, Wien-Köln-Graz 1985

Otto Antonia Graf, *Otto Wagner. 2. Das Werk des Architekten. 1903–1918*, Wien-Köln-Graz 1985

Peter Haiko (Text) – Roberto Schezen (Fotos), *Wien 1850–1930. Architektur*, Wien 1992

Géza Hajós – Eckart Vancsa, *Österreichische Kunsttopographie. Die Kunstdenkmäler Wiens. Die Profanbauten des III., IV. und V. Bezirkes*, Wien 1980

Ludwig Hevesi, *Acht Jahre Secession*, Wien 1906

Ludwig Hevesi, *Altkunst – Neukunst*, Wien 1909

Otto Kapfinger (Redaktion) - Peter Nigst (Text und Recherche), *Robert Örley*, Reihe „Portraits österreichischer Architekten", Vol. 3, ed. by Architektur Zentrum Wien, Wien - New York 1996

Otto Kapfinger, *Wiener Läden*, in: Johannes Spalt, *Portale & Geschäfte. Historische Wiener Geschäftsanlagen*, Wien-Köln-Weimar 1999

Gustav Künstler, *Zu Lois Welzenbachers Bauten*, in: Österreichs Bau- und Werkkunst, ed. by Zentralvereinigung der Architekten Österreichs, 3. Jg., Wien, Mai 1927, pp. 190–192

Heinrich Kulka (Ed.): *Adolf Loos. Das Werk des Architekten*, Wien 1931 (reprinted 1979)

Andreas Lehne, *Jugendstil in Wien. Ein Architekturführer*, Wien 1989
Joseph August Lux, Otto Wagner, Wien 1914

Ernst A. Plischke, *Ein Leben mit Architektur*, Wien 1989

Marco Pozzetto, *Max Fabiani. Ein Architekt der Monarchie*, Wien 1983

Damjan Prelovsek, *Josef Plečnik – Wiener Arbeiten von 1896 bis 1914*, Wien 1979

L. W. Rochowanski, *Josef Hoffmann. Eine Studie geschrieben zu seinem 80. Geburtstag*, Wien 1950

GLOSSARY

Burkhardt Rukschcio – Roland Schachel, *Adolf Loos. Leben und Werk*, Salzburg-Wien 1982

August Sarnitz, *Lois Welzenbacher. Architekt. 1889–1955*, Salzburg-Wien 1989

August Sarnitz, (Ed.), *Architektur Wien. 500 Bauten*, Wien-New York 1997

Eduard F. Sekler, *Josef Hoffmann. Das architektonische Werk*, Salzburg-Wien 1982

Johannes Spalt – Hermann Czech (compilation and design), *Josef Frank 1885–1967*, Exhib. cat., Hochschule für angewandte Kunst, Wien 1981

Ottokar Uhl, *Moderne Architektur in Wien von Otto Wagner bis heute*, Wien-München 1966

Helmut Weihsmann, *Das rote Wien. Sozialdemokratische Architektur und Kommunalpolitik 1919–1934*, Wien 1985

Arcade
An arch set on a supporting element (columns, pillars). This can also be an arrangement of arches.

Architrave
A horizontal beam used in antique building and other styles influenced by this approach. It supports the upper structure.

Arbor
Small, light wood garden house or a walkway immediately in front of street-side housing.

Atlas
Designations of a larger-than-life male figure that carries the structure above it; used instead of a tectonic support.

Attic
Low structure over the main eaves of a building generally finished with a cornice.

Attic apartment in the adapted part of the roof.

Attic Roof
Creased roof with a steeper incline on the bottom end.

Aula
Interior court of a Greek house, the common designation for the ceremonial hall of a school or university since the 16th century.

Axial
Lying on the axis.

Baldachin
Altar or bed canopy.

Baluster
A short pillar or column of circular or polygonal section made of stone or wood slender above and swelling into an elliptical pear-shaped ending.

Balustrade
A series of balusters surmounted by a rail or coping used on steps, bridges and balconies, etc.

Basilika
Originally an office building in Agora, Athens; an elongated hall in the Roman Empire used for markets and court sessions. It measures three to five naves or pillar and columns. It is elevated on the narrow end with space for seating. The middle nave and its high walls are generally wider and taller than transepts. Adopted by Christianity for the first churches that were built.

Bay-window
English term for a specific oriel window that is only interrupted twice within the height of the window area and not of the entire floor.

Built along the edge
Residential buildings constructed along the edges of a site.

Campo Santo
Cemetery, this term is especially applicable if a consistent shape defines the site.

Candelabra
A candle or lamp fixture made of metal, wood or stone, often monumental with a richly decorated shaft.

Capital
Projecting headpiece of a support.

Caryatid
Figure of a girl with a basket or cushion-shaped plaster headpiece used as a support instead of a tectonic strut.

Chapel Choir
Radial chapels built around a central point in a semi-circular or polygonal choir and/or choir aisle.

Choir
The area in a church reserved for the prayer of priests/monks, generally close to the altar.

Choir Aisle
An aisle encompassing the choir that is actually the continuation of the transept.

Columned Portico
Columned halls, generally on the presentation side of a building lying along the axis of the main portal, see "Portico."

Console
Projecting element, that acts as a support, a stone on which an arch, cornice, sculptures, beams, balconies, oriel rooms, services, vaulted ceiling and other similar elements are set.

Convex
A surface that curves outward rather than inward.

Cornice
Generally a horizontal construction element that structures a wall in different segments.

Crossbeam
Crossbeam.

Cube
Cube.

Eaves
Cornice under the ledge.

Edge Building
(See "Blockrandverbauung".)

Exedra
Originally a semi-circular extension of the colonnades typical of Greek

temples and public places. Also used for semi-circular building segments later.

Festoon
Arch shaped hanging ornament consisting of leaves, flowers and fruits. Often includes fluttering ribbons on both ends.

Figure Frieze
Frieze decorated with depictions of figures.

Figure-shaped aedicule
Small temple-like structure offering space for a statue.

Foyer
Anteroom.

Gable
The shape of the uppermost part of a saddle roof, also the crowning element of a window.

Gable Area
The gable surface.

Greek Cross
A form of cross with equally long ends, different to the Latin cross.

Grooves
Vertical concave grooves. Generally along the shaft of a supporting element.

Iconography
A pictorial representation.

Lateral Pediment
Corner pediment, a lateral pediment as opposed to the central pediment, see Pediment.

Ledge
Edge, the lower, horizontal border of a roof.

Lintel
Straight upper trim element on a door or window opening.

Loggia
Open, pillared room of a building. Should be enclosed by walls on five sides strictly speaking.

Main Floor
See *piano nobile*.

Middle Pediment
Pediment in the middle of a structure.

Monolith
Construction segment or structure made of a single stone (pillar).

Parapet
City wall barrier, defensive ramparts and protective walls, Later a purely decorative element crowning the wall.

Parapets
Sequence of parapets on tower or the crowning element of a building.

Partial Paneling
Wall paneling, generally made of wood and not extending over the full height of the room.

Pediment
A wide, low-pitched gable surmounting the façade of a building.

Pergola
An arbor formed of growing plants creating a garden walkway.

Piano nobile
The main floor of a building.

Pilaster
Wall column.

Pilaster-strip
Almost smooth vertical wall reinforcement without a base or capital used to strcture façades.

Porthole
Circular or elliptical window, often in the front arch of an arched structure.

Portico

A foyer or front of building generally supported by columns, pillars are also used occasionally.

Profile

Cross-section of a structural element consisting of its projection and/or recessing.

Projecting

An element that projects over the wall surfaces.

Pylon

Column tower, e.g. the struts supporting suspension bridge elements.

Pyramid Roof

Tent roof, a pyramid-shaped roof.

Roof Crest

The uppermost, generally horizontal cutting line between two diagonal roof panels.

Satellite Cupola

A smaller cupola next to the main cupola.

Shuttered Niche

A niche that is given greater emphasis by the type and color of the stone or plaster used.

Skylight

Upper middle section of a basilica's nave featuring a window to allow light to stream in, a skylight.

Supportive beam

Surface on which a supporting element (e.g. a spar) lies.

Tent Roof

Pyramid-shaped roof over a building erected on a multi-cornered or square layout, featuring a hipped roof whose surfaces come together in a pointy ending as opposed to being joined at the roof crest.

Triglyph

Three-segment frieze; triglyphs are imitation stone bulkheads.

Vestibule

Entry area of a house, possibly featuring a wardrobe.

Wall Crown

The top end of a wall.

Window Frames

The frame of a window, also trim elements along the outside edge of a window opening.

Wreath-shaped Cornice

A special form of cornice that still belongs to the outer wall in structural terms and is generally built as console ledge.

INDEX

BY BUILDING TYPE

PERSONS

SpringerArchitecture

Matthias Boeckl (ed.)

MuseumsQuartier Wien

Die Architektur / The Architecture

2001. 144 pages. Numerous figures in colour.
Format: 21 x 29,7 cm
Text: German/English
Hardcover EUR 28,90
ISBN 3-211-83641-1
Edition Architektur aktuell, Volume 3

One of the ten largest cultural complexes in the world is being created in the heart of Vienna, Austria. This spectacular connection between historic (Fischer von Erlach) and modern architecture (Ortner*Ortner) is the embodied vision of a superlative cultural statement.

This book examines not only the architecture but also the impact of such a complex undertaking.

With contributions by Friedrich Achleitner, Dieter Bogner, Bart Lootsma, Erich Raith and Matthias Boeckl.

Lavishly designed, throughout full colour, hardcover.

„Man muss das zweisprachige Buch ‚Museumsquartier Wien – Die Architektur/The Architecture' lesen … Das Buch enthält so viel kaum bekanntes historisches Material, dass es auch als Viennensium ein Muss ist …"

Die Furche

SpringerWienNewYork

A-1201 Wien, Sachsenplatz 4–6, P.O. Box 89, Fax +43.1.330 24 26, e-mail: books@springer.at, www.springer.at
D-69126 Heidelberg, Haberstraße 7, Fax +49.6221.345-229, e-mail: orders@springer.de
USA, Secaucus, NJ 07096-2485, P.O. Box 2485, Fax +1.201.348-4505, e-mail: orders@springer-ny.com
EBS, Japan, Tokyo 113, 3–13, Hongo 3-chome, Bunkyo-ku, Fax +81.3.38 18 08 64, e-mail: orders@svt-ebs.co.jp

Springer-Verlag
and the Environment